1972

PORTRAIT OF BEETHOVEN

PORTRAIT OF BEETHOVEN

An Illustrated Biography

Fritz Zobeley

Translated by Ann O'Brien

HERDER AND HERDER

1972
HERDER AND HERDER NEW YORK
232 Madison Avenue, New York 10016

Original edition: *Ludwig van Beethoven*
in Selbstzeugnissen und Bilddokumenten,
© 1965 by Rowohlt Taschenbuch Verlag GmbH,
Reinbek bei Hamburg.

Grateful acknowledgment is made to Alfred A. Knopf, Inc., for the
excerpt reprinted on page 7 from *Doctor Faustus* by Thomas Mann,
© 1948.

CONTENTS

The theme [of the arietta from op. 111] goes through a hundred vicissitudes, a hundred worlds of rhythmic contrasts, at length outgrows itself, and is finally lost in giddy heights that one might call other-worldly or abstract. And in just that very way Beethoven's art had overgrown itself, risen out of the habitable regions of tradition, even before the startled gaze of human eyes, into spheres of the entirely and utterly and nothing-but personal—an ego painfully isolated in the absolute, isolated too from sense by the loss of his hearing; lonely prince of a realm of spirits, from whom now only a chilling breath issued to terrify his most willing contemporaries, standing as they did aghast at these communications of which only at moments, only by exception, they could understand anything at all.

Thomas Mann, *Doctor Faustus*

Ludwig van Beethoven. Contemporary portrait, around 1800.

MUSIC, MY FOREMOST YOUTHFUL OCCUPATION

UNNOTICED by the world, the three "musicians" of the Beethoven family were united for a celebration—for the first and only time in their lives—on the occasion of the baptism of the youngest, Ludovic, on December 17, 1770, when the godmother, their well-to-do neighbor from the Moor Inn, carried the newborn baby from the birth chamber in the attic across Bonngasse to the church of St. Remigius. Neither the day nor hour of his birth are known, and even when he was forty years old and a musician of European fame, Ludovic considered himself to be two years younger and obstinately evaded the question of the date of his birth. It was also difficult to establish the place of his birth, since the Zülpich musicians' hospice was at one time considered a more likely location. Indeed, the confusion was such that in the encyclopedia of his time he was said to be a natural son of Frederick the Great.

There can be no doubt that fortune had not favored any of his family. At barely seventeen years of age, Maria Magdalena Keverich from Ehrenbreitstein, his mother, had been married to a valet of the Elector of Treves. The following year she bore him a son, who died shortly afterwards. And at the age of eighteen she was widowed as well. Two years later she married Johann van Beethoven, a tenor singer at the Bonn court of the Elector of Cologne. In the remaining twenty years of her life she bore him at least seven children, in spite of the lingering consumption of which she eventually died. "What is marriage?" she is once reported to have said, "a little joy followed by a chain of sorrows."

But to go back a little further in the family history: Beethoven's grandparents led a restless existence in the course of which they worked their way through the Brabant, to Malines, Louvain, Antwerp, and perhaps Maestricht, where they encountered repeated financial troubles and were forced by utter

The grandfather, Lodewyk van Beethoven. Portrait by Leopold A. Radoux, 1773.

ruin to migrate to Bonn. Certain errors stem directly from this point, in that most people overlook the fact that Brabant with its Flemish population had belonged since time immemorial to the Burgundian part of the old German Empire, as indeed it still did long after Ludwig van Beethoven had moved to Vienna. The country became Belgian only after his death. Its inhabitants are related to the Batavians, who are mentioned by the Roman historian Tacitus, and the term "Betouwe" still occurs in the name of their original settlement, an island in the Rhine between the Waal and the Lower Rhine in the vicinity of Arnhem and Nijmegen. The word stems from "bet," the root of the native word "better" (in English "beet"), and "ouwe," meaning meadow or pasture.

Over the centuries the name has been written in a variety of ways ranging from Betho, Betuwe, and Beethove to the present form, Beethoven, and it has been suggested that the indication of origin could possibly refer to the territory of Betho near Tongern. Though the final form of spelling was established as early as the time of Egmont, it is significant that even the three musicians of the family were still very free in their treatment of it.

The Catholic part of the Beethoven family presumably migrated in the course of the Reformation, to the Austrian Netherlands, where by 1700 it is known to have been flourishing, including even painters and sculptors among its ranks. The immediate predecessors of the musicians' branch of the family do not claim to be descended from these artistic ancestors, but rather from peasant and artisan stock, which can be traced back to a Johann van Bethoven, circa 1500. A certain Kornelius, born near Louvain at the end of the Thirty Years' War, chose the carpenter's trade and moved with his parents to Malines (Mecheln). His son Michael, born the year before Bach, became a master baker, and set up a fine art and lace trade next to his bakery

11

in the house of the Spotted Ox, and subsequently in the Peper-straat.

The youngest of his three sons, Ludwig van Beethoven's grandfather, Lodewyck, was born in 1712. As a small boy he sang in the choir of the local cathedral church, and was apparently trained as a professional singer, so that at nineteen he found employment as tenor singer and assistant leader of the choir at Louvain. A year later he succeeded in making the jump to the well-known orchestra at Liége. The following spring, at the age of twenty-one, he was appointed court musician at Bonn, at a salary of three hundred florins, with a raise shortly afterwards to four hundred. His eldest brother had already settled in Bonn as a merchant supplying the court with candles, and it was he who in September 1733 acted as witness at his brother's marriage to the nineteen-year-old Maria Josepha Poll, a native of the neighborhood of Cologne. The two brothers, who described themselves as citizens of Ghent, cannot have been unaware that their father's business in Malines was heading for total ruin. When their debts amounted to twelve thousand guilders, the Beethoven parents were forced to flee to friends in Celle. The two sons did not comply with an order from the jurymen of Malines to appear before the court of that city, and it is not known how the liabilities there were finally settled. In the meantime, the Bonn branch of the Beethoven family broke off all connections with their native land, though their house in Malines fell victim to the pickaxe only a few years ago.

For several years after this nothing more is heard of the achievements of the highly gifted singer, a fact which probably reflects his satisfaction at the successful change of location from the late medieval city of Malines to Bonn, an elegant residence in the French style of architecture, with its two pleasure palaces of Poppelsdorf and Brühl, furnished in the most luxurious fashion according to the plans of François Cuvilliés and Bal-

The birthplace in Bonn. A view from the garden.

thasar Neumann, and set among spacious gardens—the scenes of court festivities on which the pleasure-seeking ruler spent fifty thousand florins a year. Admittedly, he had no Johann Stamitz, no Hasse, Quantz, or Telemann in his service, and those who stood out among the ranks of court musicians from France or Munich were at most virtuosos on the violin or cello.

Some years later, in about 1740, Ludwig's two first children having died in infancy, and his parents having in the meantime sought a final refuge in Bonn, another son was born and was christened Johann. From this time onwards, there are increasing reports about the court orchestra. Shortly after this there appeared Touchemoulin, a violinist from Châlons who had been trained under Tartini at the court's expense. Other court musicians are also mentioned—Salomon, Ries, van den Eeden—who were all to play a part in the life of the young Beethoven. The entire repertoire was still closely based on the needs of the court: carnival operas, Lenten oratorios, name-day cantatas, and church music; music for table, court concerts and serenades, as well as some chamber music in the apartments of the prince himself. Clearly defined contracts stipulated the duties of service; obedience and constant readiness even to make journeys to any one of the Elector's half-dozen other residences were essential. As solo singer Lodewyck would have been given important parts, such as that of Adamo in the oratorio *La morte d'Abel*. In addition to this he was entrusted with teaching the youths placed in his charge. He must have been able to play the harpsicord, and perhaps even one or more other instruments as well.

He could teach his own son no more than this by the time the boy, in addition to attending first the primary and then the Latin (secondary) schools, began to follow in his father's footsteps. At the age of ten Johann was already taking part in the Jesuit plays. Two years later he was named a candidate for the court orchestra, and at sixteen was even appointed a court musician. Originally active with the orchestra as singer, he was also employed as a violinist.

The situation could not be expected to improve except by a change of ruler, which in fact occurred when the Elector literally danced his way into eternity by overexhausting himself at a ball in 1761. Since the House of Wittelsbach could produce no claimant, the cathedral chapter agreed with remarkable speed on Count Maximilian Friedrich von Königsegg, who was already in his sixties. No one would have predicted that he was to wear the pallium for almost a quarter of a century. He entrusted the business of government to the much-experienced Freiherr von Belderbusch, whom he appointed his Court Minister. His first step to demonstrate to the chapter his ability to economize was to reduce the fees for artists. When Touchemoulin received only four hundred instead of his usual thousand florins, he rapidly found himself a new appointment in Regensburg with the brother of the previous Elector. For want of anyone better, Lodewyck van Beethoven succeeded in obtaining the post, almost certainly with the stipulation that he continue his duties as singer, and was invested with the powers necessary to preside over the ensemble of singers and musicians.

In the memoirs of Gottfried Fischer, for many years landlord to Johann van Beethoven, we read that Johann took advantage of his father's occasional absence to make trips to Cologne, Deutz, Andernach, Koblenz, and Ehrenbreitstein. It was in fact in a tavern in Ehrenbreitstein that he made the acquaintance of the young widow Laym, née Keverich, whom he then married in November 1767. Their first son, baptized Ludwig Maria, died only six days after birth; their second son, Ludovicus, was born presumably on December 16, 1770, and baptized the week before Christmas. Four years later, in their new apartment, "Am Dreieck" (at the triangle), there followed the birth of Kaspar Karl; and two years later still that of Nikolaus Johann, in the Fischer house. Three other children died in infancy. According to

Baptismal entry from the Church of St. Remigius, December 17, 1770.

the Fischer chronicle, Ludwig was afflicted for a long time in his youth with an "infirmity" which his mother cured by home medicines. It cannot be ruled out that this was an early manifestation of the infection which ultimately caused the subsequent outbreak of "neuritis nervi acustici" and thus lay at the root of his gradually developing deafness.

Ludwig lived near his paternal grandfather, and even if his memories of him perhaps stem more from his meditations on Radoux's fine portrait of the respected musical director, the young boy's early ideal could well have been to emulate him. The old man is known to have appeared for the last time as a singer in the cantata by Lucchesi given in honor of the Elector's birthday in May 1773, and is thought to have died suddenly on Christmas Eve of the same year. The small wine trade which he had pursued for years as a sideline, buying Rhine wines from local vineyards and selling them at a profit in his native Brabant, is reputed to have led to alcoholism of both his wife and, in later years, of his son as well.

Since Johann van Beethoven was a popular music teacher, his son was tempted quite early to try his hand at the keyboard. His interest and feeling for tone and note was soon confirmed, and as he himself commented, "right from my fourth year, music began to become my foremost youthful occupation." A relation of his mother, the court musician Rovantini, taught him the violin, and there is frequent mention of both the organ and early viola playing, though it was only after Johann's death that the legend arose that "the drunken father used to pull the sleeping child from his bed to the piano where he would be tortured with exercises until the early hours of the morning."

In the meantime, Ludwig attended the elementary school, from which he long retained a memory of the bowdlerized singsong "Herr Pastorum gens bigatum." From there he went on to the Münsterschule, which he left early in order to devote himself more intensively to his "gracious muse." His first concert appearance playing "a variety of clavier concertos and trios" together with a singing pupil of his father's took place on March 26, 1778, in the hall of the music academy in Cologne, both performers having previously "had the grace to perform for the pleasure of the whole court." In reality his little son was not six years old, as his father claimed, but seven. We can trust Fischer's reliable accounts of the numerous invitations received by the father and his talented son from music lovers in the neighborhood as well as much farther afield. After a journey to Rotterdam with his mother turned out to be nothing more than a visit to relations, there is reason to suppose that he was offered a training at the court's expense, either at the express wish of, or at all events with the approval of the Elector. The harpsicord was chosen as chief instrument, and the old court organist van Eeden was appointed the boy's teacher. When he fell ill, his place was taken by Tobias F. Pfeiffer, until van den Eeden's death in 1781, when Beethoven's further education was entrusted to the new court organist, Christian Gottlob Neefe. Through the instruction he received from the Franciscan monk Willibald Koch and the Minorite father Hanzmann, he became familiar with the rites of church services.

There is no reason to doubt that his imagination developed at a very early age; his father is supposed to have tried to restrain Beethoven's premature extemporizing by asking him to try to "write down the harmonies of his soul." He was tempted to imitate whatever came into his hands, especially compositions by Sterkel. It is impossible to draw a clear distinction between the various sources of influence, such as Neefe, due to the closeness of style of the bulk of works already composed, performed, and published at the time by Neefe. These included operas, musicals, serenades, and countless piano sonatas. Neefe was a man of culture and a trained lawyer, who had been brought up with

Christian Gottlieb Neefe. Anonymous oil portrait.

a reverence for the works of C. P. E. and J. S. Bach. He had had
to flee Frankfurt on account of debts, and was appointed at a
good salary to the combined post of court organist and co-
accountant to the Bonn theater group. He must have recognized
immediately the unusual talent of the pupil entrusted to him,
and when his frequent absence from Bonn made it necessary for
him to find someone to deputize for him at his duties as organist,
his choice turned naturally to the young Beethoven. When in
1783 Lucchesi's absence created a vacancy for a harpsicordist in
the theater orchestra, Neefe saw his opportunity to complete
Beethoven's training as an accompanist. And it was also Neefe
who, in his report on the state of musical life in Bonn which
appeared in the widely circulated *Magazin der Musik,* first mentioned Mozart's name in connection with Beethoven's: "Louis

van Beethoven . . . a boy of most promising talent . . . He plays chiefly the well-tempered clavier of Sebastian Bach. Herr Neefe has also given him instruction in the continuo. He is now training him in composition. . . . This young genius deserves the support he needs to enable him to travel. He will certainly become a second Wolfgang Amadeus Mozart if he continues to make progress as he has done so far." Beethoven's first compositions date from this time, and Neefe was soon able to announce, to his delight, the publication of variations on a march by Dressler, of which the bass structure was to find its apotheosis three decades later in the Seventh Symphony—the "Maestoso" theme.

These were followed shortly afterwards by the three sonatas dedicated to the Elector Maxmilian Friedrich. In terms of theme, structure, and harmony—as was to be expected—these were a synthesis of familiar sounds and original ideas, with the typical characteristics of a march; sentimentality, fleetingness, and a forestalling energy.

Neefe on several other occasions used his connections with publishing houses to publish Beethoven's small compositions— rondos for the clavier and songs very much in the manner of his own—so that by the time he was fourteen years old he already had eight published works to his name, even if he did subsequently dismiss them, along with another fifty or so, as the sins of his youth. Since Neefe admitted that he himself had received no formal musical training, it is safe to say that his influence on the young genius lay mainly in the encouragement he gave him, and the way he spurred him on by his own example. And although Beethoven did write later to him: "If I ever become

19

famous, you too will have a share in it," we should not overlook
the cautious undertone; Beethoven was far more concerned with
acquiring the security of a comprehensive knowledge of musical
theory. Despite the fact that Neefe did restrict Beethoven's earn-
ings, allowing him to work only so far as his other activities
would permit, he did give him instruction in the continuo and
unquestionably gave his pupil every assistance in his power. One
such instance was the occasion of his "test" for the post of assistant court organist in 1784. Beethoven took the opportunity

Beethoven at the age of sixteen. Silhouette by Josef Neesen, 1786.

of its favorable outcome to ask for both a salary and a civil service promotion, to which he received the laconic but prophetic reply: "Let the matter rest."

A VERY PROMISING TALENT

LESS than two months later the Elector himself went to his rest, and forever. The question of the succession had, however, been settled four years previously, the new Elector being Maximilian Franz, the youngest son of Maria Theresa, and brother of Joseph II and the Queen of France. He had for years been Master of the Teutonic Order and Prince Archbishop of Münster, and was the first Hapsburg to sit on this throne. His maxim, influenced by Frederick the Great, was known to be: "To rule country and people is an office, a service to the state." Since Belderbusch had also just died, Maximilian intended to conduct the business of government himself. The report he ordered on staff matters led to the rapid dismissal of the theatrical society, and it is quite probable that he wanted to have Mozart as his musical director. He had known him since childhood—a picture of Mozart in 1726 showed him in the Archduke's gala robes—and the composer had staged a performance of *Il re pastore* in Maximilian's honor in April 1775 on his return to Salzburg from his sister's wedding in Paris. If we assume that he made use of his stay in Vienna to obtain Mozart's agreement, the composer must have had some reason for his refusal. Possibly Mozart was enticed by the hope of obtaining a libretto from Da Ponte, or he may have hoped for a position in the service of the Emperor. Consequently, Maximilian left the court orchestra largely unchanged. The young Beethoven appeared in the new list as "assistant court

21

organist" with a salary of one hundred and fifty florins, while his father received three hundred florins and Neefe only two hundred.

According to Fischer's description, Beethoven could then be seen striding to work in a sea-green tailcoat, short green trousers with buckles, silk stockings, and a white silk waistcoat decorated with a floral motif. He wore his hair in curls with a pigtail behind, and carried an opera hat and a sword complete with belt. He always walked bent slightly forward.

The terms of his service left him enough free time to continue his studies with Neefe, as well as for lessons with a certain Zambona or Zamponi who taught him Latin, French, Italian, and logic for at least a year. Since Neefe found himself confined exclusively to his duties as court organist, Beethoven probably had only occasional opportunity to devote himself to chamber music, which would seem to account for his relatively meager output in that genre. Indeed, it is represented only by three songs, a subsequently reworked prelude in the style of J. S. Bach, a piano concerto completely in the vein of Sterkel, and three "Quators pour le Clavecin" in the "mannered Mannheim style of Mozart," full of dynamic eccentricity, though betraying no trace of Beethoven himself. This was the sum total of his output in the peaceful years from 1784 to 1787, unless we are to assume that any other works of this period were all either lost or destroyed.

He must have found other interests to occupy him, perhaps in friendships such as that with Franz Wegeler, a medical student five years his senior who introduced him to the von Breuning family. It is also known that he had personal contact with some of the members of the orchestra, including the Romberg cousins, the two Reichas, as well as Ries and Simrock, all famous musicians who were greatly esteemed. No doubt after that Beethoven played frequently with them and his father—both privately and

Mozart's apartment in the Camesina House, Domgasse 5, Vienna, 1787.

in public. His skill on the keyboard more than qualified him for recommendation as piano teacher to the aristocratic families of the court. Many years later Beethoven himself wrote what amounts to a resumé of this year in a letter to a young musician discontented with the conditions of his studies: ". . . without by any means wishing to present myself to you as a typical example, I can assure you that I lived in a small, insignificant place and that almost everything I have become either there or here has been solely as a result of my own efforts . . ."

At the opening of the new season the Elector had engaged a different theatrical troupe, which was then soon joined by the French troupe when it became free due to the death of the Elector of Cassel. The Bonn repertoire then extended from Glück's *Alcide* and Holzbauer's *Günther von Schwarzburg* to the operas of Sachini, Paisiello, Salieri, and Grétry.

Nothing more is heard of Beethoven until the Elector finally allowed him to go to Vienna in 1787, though under what conditions or with what money is not known. He arrived on Easter Saturday, and at a festival performance of a Guglielmi opera the following day he seems to have received his first, unforgettable, and much-quoted impression of the Emperor. If it was his aim to be taken on as a pupil by Mozart, he could not have chosen a more inappropriate moment for his visit; in January Mozart had been in Prague with Constanze, giving concerts and the triumphant premiere of *The Marriage of Figaro,* and on returning to Vienna in February he brought with him the commission for a new opera. Having just completed the two great quintets, he was considering a trip to England when his father became fatally ill and he was forced to abandon the plan. And at precisely the moment when Beethoven came to call on him in his charming apartment in the Carmesian house, he was holding Da Ponte's libretto for *Don Giovanni* in his hands. But he listened to the playing of the boy, who had almost certainly been warmly recommended to him.

Mozart is reputed to have thought that Beethoven's first improvisation was a showpiece prepared and learned by heart for the occasion. It was only on hearing Beethoven's treatment of a chromatic theme which he himself proposed that he burst out with the famous statement: "Keep your eye on him, one day he will give the world something to talk about!" According to Ries, a later pupil of Beethoven, and according to a conversation recorded by Beethoven himself, there is reason to believe that he did in fact receive some instruction from Mozart during the two weeks (April 7–20) he spent in Vienna. Illness and financial problems befell him on the return trip. An episcopal councilor, Dr. von Schaden, had to lend him the thirty-five florins necessary to enable him to continue his journey which, as the Elector later learned, he was not able to pay back immediately.

The news that his mother was dangerously ill is thought to have been the real cause for his premature return to Bonn. A few weeks later, on July 17, Madame van Beethoven died. In September of the same year he wrote to the councilor in Augsburg: "My good, lovable mother . . . my happiness and my health both began to fade when she went . . . Oh, who could have been happier than I when I was still able to pronounce the sweet name of 'Mother,' and it was heard? To whom can I say it now? To the silent images that my imagination conjures up? Ever since my return I have spent few enjoyable hours; for the whole time I have been plagued with asthma, and I fear that this may even develop into consumption. I have also been suffering from melancholia . . . imagine yourself in my position . . . Fortune does not favor me here in Bonn."

His father found it necessary to ask the Elector for a considerable advance immediately after his wife's death, and so his son's simultaneous request for a salary increase, needless to say, was turned down. When his father began to drown his sorrow in the taverns, Ludwig only just managed to prevent a threatened disciplinary transfer, and secured half of his father's salary for the education of his brothers. Under such conditions, any planned return to Mozart and study in Vienna was for the time being clearly unthinkable.

We know nothing of how the house was run after the death of the mother. From letters Beethoven wrote years later to Wegeler and Eleonore von Breuning we learn that he seems to have found a new home in the von Breuning family, who seemed to understand his frequent moods and strange habits, and no doubt gave him whatever help he needed. Employed at first by Frau Hofrätin von Breuning as piano teacher, he soon became friends with her children—her daughter Elenonore, and her three sons Stephan, Christoph, and Lorenz (Lenz)—and through them he became acquainted with a stimulating circle of people who soon began to meet in Widow Koch's restaurant "Zehrgarten." In both places the chief topic of interest was contemporary literature, and with friends from the Zehrgarten circle Beethoven even matriculated in the university in 1789 to hear lectures on philosophy and literature. In this same circle he got

The marketplace in Bonn; the restaurant "Zehrgarten" is at the right. Engraving by Hundshagen.

to know a certain Count Waldstein, who was currently applying for membership in the Teutonic Order. He was a well-educated dilettante who took Beethoven under his wing, and may have interceded for him with the Elector.

Apart from this we know only of the visit to Bonn of the Mainz musical director, Righini, who was a popular composer of the day, though there is no record of a possible meeting with Beethoven. Then there is the account of the young court organist's improvised fantasies on the organ at Marienforst near Godesberg, and also of a high-spirited prank to throw one of the singers in the church choir off key, which earned him a sharp rebuke from the Elector.

On hearing of the death of the Emperor he composed an astonishingly extensive cantata in which the musical train of thought indicates a development that could result only from hours of quiet, independent work. Six months later he composed another cantata to commemorate the accession of Leopold II. Neither of these early pieces was performed.

With the arrival of 1789 the court circles were shaken by the alarming political news from France. Passing through Bonn on his way to London, Haydn was feted with a performance of one of his masses, after which he was presented by the Elector to the members of the court orchestra. Although a new directory of musicians in Bonn noted, among other things, that Beethoven played piano concertos, his name was not specifically included among the virtuosos or composers. It seems that he had no rank as such, and it is quite possible that someone who envied Beethoven's brilliance passed on to the Elector any information likely to harm his standing at the court: his father's unpleasant lawsuits against the deceased Minister von Belderbusch; the alcoholism of both his father and grandmother; the debts resulting from the trip to Vienna; the complaints of the singer he had tricked; perhaps also the language with which Beethoven defended himself; and finally the complaint that his cantatas were impossible to perform.

Although a certain amount of revolutionary skirmishing was already going on—in the neighborhood of Liége, for instance—the banquets in Bonn appear to have continued as if totally unconcerned. So, for example, we hear of festivities in the Redoutensaal on the Sunday before Mardi Gras of 1791, when a ballet was staged in period costume; its motif was "The Penchant of Our Ancestors for War, Hunting, and Carousing." The ostensible author was Waldstein, but in reality it was Ludwig van Beethoven who composed the music. Only once do we hear of him playing for Maximilian Franz, when he accompanied Ries and Romberg in a new trio by Pleyel. He had to sight-read, and although he had to wangle his way skillfully through several wrong notes, he probably received an envious glance from his master. In September of the same year Maximilian Franz organized an entire week of festivities at his residence at Mergentheim. The merry river trip, on which the Elector himself was not present, was interrupted in Aschaffenburg in order for them to hear the famous clavecin player, Abbé Sterkel. Since Beethoven's sole publication of these years, his Variations in D major on Righini's air *Venni amore,* had just appeared, he was called upon to give an immediate demonstration of his capacity as a virtuoso. Any doubts Abbé Sterkel may have harbored were instantly dispelled, and replaced by his greatest admiration and untiring praise. In Mergentheim, however, Beethoven stubbornly refused to play in public—as was to occur so frequently in later years—ostensibly on account of the inferior instrument. Subsequently, though, he played to a private circle, extemporizing from a seemingly inexhaustible wealth of ideas.

He had scarcely returned to Bonn when he was deeply shocked by the news of Mozart's death. "Who will console the world at

Baroness Maria Anna Wilhelmine von Westerholt.

this loss?" he is reputed to have said. Only Wegeler, his friends in the von Breuning household, his charming pupil Fräulein von Westerholt, or his passionately adored Eleonore von Breuning can have had an inkling of all that he had composed since his return from Vienna. It amounted to over two dozen works, excluding the two cantatas already mentioned and the songs and arias for the Ritter ballet; chamber music such as the duos for clarinet and bassoon, the octet for wind instruments, and string trios. Though this may not have been a very large output, it showed the promise of things to come. Influential patrons such as Countess Hatzfeld and Countess Wolff-Metternich had long since taken note of the talented young man.

After the thwarted attempt to escape made by Louis XVI and Marie Antoinette, and after the dissolution of the Austro-French Alliance, combined with the preparations being made for military intervention in France, it is easily understandable that a ruler in such an exposed position as the Elector of Cologne

Joseph Haydn. Watercolor drawing after John Hoppner by Georg Sigismund Facius, 1971.

should have been beset with problems other than the musical entertainment of his court. Yet even in the midst of these troubles Maximilian Franz never neglected his duties as an art-loving ruler, for he granted scholarships to two painters, the von Kügelgen brothers, for a study visit to Italy. This may have raised Beethoven's own hopes for such an opportunity. Since Haydn was the only possible teacher, the assistant court organist must have concentrated all his hopes on the famous composer's return from London in March 1792. However, the Elector's brother, Emperor Leopold, had died in March of that year, so that Maximilian Franz was in Frankfurt to attend the imperial elections when Haydn arrived in Bonn. The court orchestra held a breakfast in his honor in Godesberg, and it was probably on that occasion that one of Beethoven's cantatas was slipped into Haydn's hands as proof of his talent. As Hadyn then proceeded immediately on to Frankfurt, where he met Count Esterhazy and possibly the Elector as well, the decision concerning Beethoven's future could well have been taken either there or soon afterwards in Vienna.

All we know is that at midnight on August 23, Beethoven wrote a duet for two flutes for one of his friends in Bonn, apparently as a memento, and that shortly after this the Zehrgarten circle hurriedly compiled a little autogram album for him, in which the last contribution is dated November 1, 1792. It is a volume of poetry full of farewell greetings, as for instance Count Waldstein's well-known, prophetic words: "Through continuous hard work you will receive Mozart's spirit from the hands of Haydn." Although we have no definite information to prove that Waldstein was in fact the anonymous financial donor who made it possible for Beethoven to study in Vienna, there can be no doubt that he gave him several letters of introduction. As Beethoven himself wrote over thirty years later in a message to an unknown pianist: "A capable fellow needs nothing but the rec-

31

ommendation from the right people to the right people." Most of the families in Vienna who opened their doors to him in this way were close relations of Count Waldstein.

THE GENERAL ART OF MUSIC

THE coach carrying Beethoven and the Bonn oboist, Libisch, hurried right through the already marching Hessian army, and eventually arrived at Vienna. Though he could not have realized it at the time, this journey was to result in his settling permanently in Vienna, just as his grandfather before him had once moved from Malines via Liége to Bonn. To the end of his life he often hoped and planned to "see again my native land, that beautiful country where I first saw the light of day," and once even spoke of wanting to "feel the soil of Brabant under my feet and to see the graves of my ancestors"—despite the fact that three of his grandparents came from the Moselle-Middle Rhine district. His stay in Vienna, for which the Elector allowed him 500 florins over and above his current expenses, was apparently initially planned to last for one year. Once in Vienna, Libisch parted company with his traveling companion, and at the completion of his year's studies returned home to the court orchestra in Bonn. Beethoven, on the other hand, began his lessons with Haydn. Entries in his diary soon run: "Haidn eight Groschen" or "Twenty-two Kreuzer for Haidn, and a hot chocolate for me."

Barely six weeks after his departure from Bonn he received the shattering news of his father's death. "The drinking tax . . . has suffered a loss" was Waldstein's sole comment. In Bonn Franz Ries, the violinist and a friend of the family, undertook to deal with the inheritance and probably with the fate of Beethoven's younger brothers as well. Karl seems to have prepared himself for a career as a civil servant, while Johann served his apprenticeship in the court pharmacy. The Elector had left Bonn at the same time as Beethoven, and was able to return there only briefly, from April to September 1793, before being banished for good. For the time being Beethoven was provided with adequate resources, and a room was found for him in one of Prince Lichnowsky's houses.

Beethoven's counterpoint exercises from his student days—of which two hundred and forty-five of the original three hundred have been preserved—indicate a somewhat systematic curriculum. He also paid several visits each week to Schuppanzigh—not the sixteen-year-old Ignaz who was about to change from the viola to the violin, but his father, who taught Beethoven enough Italian to enable him to take lessons with Salieri. It is characteristic of Beethoven's enthusiasm and resoluteness that before long he was blaming Haydn whenever any mistake was left uncorrected —whether inadvertently or because the older man was overburdened with his own work. Because of this Beethoven also took secret lessons from Johann Schenk, a successful composer of musical comedies, who had had the benefit of a thorough musical training and knew how to impart it to Beethoven. Quite apart from this the news of the young musician's skill on the piano must have spread rapidly, and he did not lack opportunities to enter houses of the nobility, as Haydn himself confirmed.

Toward the close of the year's lessons, Haydn felt obliged to submit a report to the Elector, which he did in the form of a letter dated November 23, 1793. "Expert and non-expert alike must . . . without prejudice admit that in time Beethoven will become one of the greatest musicians in Europe, and I shall be proud to be able to call myself his teacher . . . " Beethoven also included a few lines of his own, remarking that he had not per-

The Alstergasse, seen from Beethoven's first apartment in Vienna.

mitted himself much composition, in order to devote all his mental powers to "the general art of music." Haydn also inserted five compositions—possibly without Beethoven's knowledge. The comment that his pupil was barely able to exist on the money allowed him enraged the Elector, who replied that he already knew all but one of the enclosed compositions from Bonn, and that this one piece could hardly be proof of the progress made in Vienna. Fearing that Beethoven, "as on his first trip to Vienna, would bring nothing but debts back with him," he somewhat ungraciously requested "whether he could not begin his journey back to Bonn, so that he can fulfill his duties here" (December 23, 1793).

But exactly a month later the Elector himself was in Vienna once more, just in time to see Haydn before he set out on his second visit to England. It may originally have been planned that

Beethoven should accompany him on the journey, but the necessary consent seems to have been withheld. In any event, Marie Antoinette having been guillotined at the hands of the Revolution, the Elector was beset with far greater worries than the finishing touches of the training of his assistant court organist. He must, however, have given his approval to another year's study in Vienna, but this time—in the absence of Haydn—with Albrechtsberger, a skilled theoretician. From the "Münster Court Plan" of 1794, written in the Elector's own handwriting, we learn that Beethoven was to "remain without salary in Vienna until he is called back [to Münster]," thus proving that he still belonged, as before, to the ranks of the court orchestra. Yet Maximilian Franz could hardly have left him entirely without money.

In contrast to Haydn, Albrechtsberger took his duties very

seriously, and the number of exercises Beethoven did under his supervision demonstrates that the eighteen months of study provided him with considerable self-confidence in his command of the techniques of composition. Bearing in mind the pupil's pronounced rebelliousness, on which all his teachers were agreed, Beethoven's own comment of more than twenty years later bears more weight than all the malicious scandal-mongering and distortion: "I have lost my Albrechtsberger and can trust no one else," even if he could turn around and mock "the art of creating musical skeletons." Among the acquaintances he had already made through his reputation as a piano virtuoso was Baron van Swieten, the son of Maria Theresa's personal physician, who was

Prince Karl Lichnowsky. Oil portrait, by F. Gödel.

also an intimate friend of the Elector of Cologne. He was known as the Viennese "pope of music," and was a great lover of older music, especially Bach and Handel. An early letter in his handwriting to Beethoven already shows signs of the utmost familiarity, where the latter is asked to present himself "at half past eight in the evening, with his sleeping cap in a bag." As Mozart before him, Beethoven became acquainted with Handel's oratorios and operas here.

Strangely enough, Beethoven did not name Prince Lichnowsky, with whom he lived, as "premier Mécene de sa Muse" but a certain Count von Browne-Camus. To this man and his wife he dedicated no fewer than seven works, including the Piano Sonata op. 22 known as "The Swans" after a novel by Griepenkerl of 1838. His relationship with the Browne family came to an end with the premature death of the countess in 1803. The number of his patrons became publicly known through the list of subscribers to his op. 1 of 1795, which included such names as Kinsky, Liechtenstein, Palfy-Erdödy, Thun, Schönborn, Lobkowitz, Esterházy, for the greater part close relations of Count Waldstein. Many of them remained closely bound to Beethoven for the rest of his life. In 1793 Haydn introduced him into the Esterházy family, and it was in their house that Beethoven was undoubtedly introduced into a society in which his skill at improvisation and his piano compositions soon won him admirers. He may well have been discreetly rewarded for any dedications he made, for playing in private concerts, as well as for piano instruction, but in 1794 he still remained on the Bonn payment list at a salary of 600 florins.

His period of instruction with Hadyn lasted a year, that with Schenk six months, and that with Albrechtsberger until the spring of 1795. The consultations with Salieri and E. A. Förster took place only occasionally, and it is assumed that his connections with Maximilian Franz must have come to an end at about this time. The insignificant court musician from Bonn thus became an independent Viennese piano virtuoso and composer, who from this time on had to ensure himself an income from his own work.

MY SPIRIT SHALL STILL PREVAIL

HIS desk had long been piled high with books full of sketches and notes, not only those dating from Bonn days, but also some plans made during his three years in Vienna. Such works as he had completed differed from his old "dinner-table contributions" in that they conformed to the independent Viennese traditions and also offered him scope to demonstrate his own particular brilliance. Although certain editions contain far more cycles of variations, the sequence of works provided with opus numbers, beginning with the piano trios mentioned above, serves to indicate the "legitimate" as against the incidental compositions. Only three other variations appeared before the publication of this op. 1, but it is thought that other works previously were circulated in manuscript form, as is known to have been so in the case of the String Trio in E-flat major op. 3. If the original manuscripts of many early works have been lost, the same fate may have befallen the copies. Beethoven's sense of responsibility now demanded that he revise all his earlier works if they were to be included in the list of works bearing opus numbers. Of the works published in the following five years, about half were not included in this list. A glance reveals that these omitted works approximated his "Salon Repertoire," in particular his "Variations pour le Clavecin." They are extremely interesting for us, as they show how Beethoven the improviser was influenced by the appreciative applause of his audiences. Although the genre itself did not present him with any formal problems to speak of, it did offer him the opportunity of testing the dexterity of his fingering, his skill at characterization, at shaping contrasts, his elegance of wit and the richness of his imagination—in short his "rhetorical" abilities. Although the principle of the variation is very old, and examples of it abound, the "modern" variations of Haydn and Mozart became the first models for the stereotype compositions of their lesser contemporaries, and Beethoven managed to retrieve them and develop them further.

Though Beethoven knew himself to be totally superior to this "salon art," he seems to have encountered certain difficulties in his program of chamber music compositions. This made itself evident in the form of indecision. He reworked his Octet for Wind Instruments as a string quintet; in op. 16 the wind instruments may be replaced by strings. Correspondingly, the final version of his first piano concerto was composed in fact after the second, so we do not even know for sure with which of the piano concertos Beethoven made his concert debut. All that is definite is that it was on March 29 at a concert in the Burgtheater conducted by Salieri, and that the soloist was announced as "the virtuoso, Ludwig van Beethoven." It is not inconceivable that only the scores of the orchestra were completed and that he himself had to improvise his own part to a very large extent. In the second concert under Salieri the following day, a specific item of the program was reserved for Beethoven's free improvisation, with which he created the greatest sensation. The next day, in the interval of a charity performance of *La clemenza di Tito* in aid of Mozart's widow, he played Mozart's Piano Concerto in D minor (K 466) which was a particular favorite of his, and which he later embellished with his own cadences. The only report of these concerts on record is that they were met with the "unanimous applause of the audience."

Participating in concerts, invited into the salons of the princes, counts, and wealthy citizens of Vienna, instructing fashionable ladies of the aristocracy, sketching and executing his compositions, supervising the copyists and correcting manuscripts for printing: thus we can imagine the occupation of his days, weeks, and months during the years that followed. An entry in the journal he began on his departure from Bonn seems particularly apt: "Courage, regardless of any weaknesses of my body, my spirit shall still prevail; they have been there for twenty-three years; this year the complete man must be decided, nothing may be left undone." The only difference is that by then Beethoven was twenty-five.

Just after these concerts he signed the contract with Artaria who, on an advance payment of two hundred and twelve florins, agreed to publish his op. 1, the three piano trios dedicated to Prince Lichnowsky. The issue of subscriptions led to an immediate order of two hundred and fifty copies. Of the success of this work there can be no better proof than the numerous reprints of it by other publishers. In the course of thirty or forty years no fewer than twenty editions were published. The note on the printed piano score, "For the pianoforte with accompaniment," refers to a form of musicmaking which enjoyed great popularity among amateur groups: the "Sonate avec Accompagnement d'un Violin et Violoncelle (obligé or ad libitum)." The contribution of the strings was restricted for lines on end to nothing but monotonous accompanying chords, the divisions of chords and repetition, as is found even in Beethoven's first violin and cello sonatas, and scarcely to the undivided joy of the players. But players and listeners alike must have been aware of the grip of the new maestro in his op. 1. The twelve movements of these early trios differ from later examples of the form not so much through their verve, richness of thought, and thematic coherence as through their traditional construction. It is well known that Beethoven was annoyed by Haydn's advice not to publish the third Trio in C minor for the time being. His pupil Ries explained that the well-meaning teacher had said this not out of displeasure or envy, but because he wanted to spare Beethoven any possible shock effects. But it was precisely in this trio that the totally new and characteristic quality of his music found its most striking expression. With this debut Beethoven began in the eyes of his contemporaries to enter into the heritage of Mozart. He himself must have been aware that at least his friends and patrons would in future be expecting him to compose in all forms—from piano sonatas to symphonies, operas, oratorios, and masses.

The sonata for piano, violin, and cello and above all the string quartet were standard types of the chamber music repertoire. Though Beethoven was probably more familiar with mixed ensembles including wind instruments, his rondos, duos, and serenades still radiate the lightheartedness of the old divertimento, full of Baroque relics and Salzburgian respectability; fine, clear compositions still worthy of being played.

But this was frankly not what was expected of him here in Vienna, with its sophisticated customs. His rank as a piano virtuoso made it fully understandable that he should first think of his own instrument; for it he composed dances and minuets, sonatas, countless variations, sonatinas and little serenades for the encouragement of his pupils. His work at this time clearly incorporated a veritable hoard of chamber music, including the Quintet for Wind Instruments op. 16, the instantly popular Septet in E-flat major op. 20, three violin sonatas as well as two for cello and one for horn; and also some unusual pieces such as the Sonatina and Adagio in F minor for Mandolin and Harpsichord. Then there were the string trios: op. 3, the Trio in E-flat major; the Senerade in D op. 8; and the three Trios of op. 9, especially the mysterious third, again in C minor. Its quality may best be summed up in the term coined for *Fidelio,* that whereas other works may be amusing or entertaining, this trio "allows one no sleep."

Shortly after this, Beethoven's interest began to shift to the more demanding larger forms, though to start with, of course, only in draft form. He touched up yet again the First Piano Concerto, completed the Third, and even before finishing the First Symphony the Six String Quartets of op. 18 were ready for performance. If the majority of Italian arias, duets, and scenes composed at this time are dismissed as "the fruits of his studies," some of his vocal creations of these years are quite outstanding; among them we find for instance the song "Adelaide" and the settings of such texts as "Der Freie Mann" by G. C. Pfeffel, which are thought to have inspired him like "The Sighs of an Unhappy Lover" and "Mutual Love," not so much by their language as by their programmatic content. Most of these songs were undoubtedly given their premiere by some celebrated soprano or virtuoso in the salons of his patrons or at a subscription concert very soon after they were completed. Whereas the number of publications in the twelve years from the time of the *Dressler* Variations (1782/83) up to the completion of his studies amounted to only twelve, a total of thirty-five publications followed in the period 1795–1800, including many which in turn contained two or three fully developed works. But these were not merely points of departure from the achievements of his predecessors: the continual confrontation with his striking ideas and his particular ability to express them singled him out uniquely from the ranks of his contemporaries.

We have, however, no such abundant documentation as to the circumstances of his private life. Contact with his native Rhineland was maintained through correspondence; he exchanged gifts with "Lorchen"—a cravat in exchange for a composition. And any differences that may have existed were made up with Simrock and Wegeler. The decisive poles of his character emerge from his hastily jotted notes; on the one hand a good-natured sense of humor combined with a delight in punning and wordplay, aversion to any kind of formality; and on the other hand the resoluteness never to allow any shadow to obscure the purity of his convictions. Thus we find him uttering fiery exclamations such as: "Don't let him ever come near me again! He is a false dog . . .," which he would retract hastily the following day with some such remark as: "My dear fellow! You are a sincere chap, and you were quite right . . ." One of his most loyal friends, Nikolaus Zmeskall, soon appears addressed as: "Dear Baron Muckraker . . . Go to the devil, I don't want to hear another word of your ideas on morality. Power is the morality of those who distinguish themselves above others, and so it is for me . . ."

In response to requests and "out of love for the affinity that exists between the arts," he composed the first of his many dances for the winter ball of the Society of Artists. It was to be the first of over a hundred compositions in that form. Though the Viennese beauties—according to the *Zeitung für die elegante Welt,* the society newspaper—had been complaining for years about the boredom of the minuet, Beethoven's were singled out as "simple, pleasant, and original." In December 1795 and January 1796 he appeared frequently at the keyboard in public.

He then gave up his apartment in order to travel, and by February was already in Prague as companion to Prince Lichnowsky. The fact that there is no documented record of any performances in Prague in no way proves anything about his actual activities during his stay. Indeed, Mozart's academy concert of ten years previously is substantiated solely by one chance letter in his own hand. Beethoven certainly did not lack admirers there, as is proven by the list of subscribers for his op. 1, of which a not inconsiderable number of copies were bound for Prague. His next destination, Dresden, is confirmed by a letter from the former court marshall at Bonn to Maximilian Franz: "Young Beethoven arrived here yesterday . . . He is said to have improved enormously and to be able to compose well" (April 24). In the meantime some of his latest works had appeared.

One of the letters of recommendation he had brought with him gained him access to court circles. Before his first audience, which was planned to include a short concert, could take place —the court was currently in mourning—the Elector learned that "all who heard him play the piano were in raptures," and that even the Elector of Sachsen, himself a "connoisseur of music . . . was exceptionally pleased with him" and had given him a gold snuff box. Beethoven for his part sent his compliments to "My distant Grace," but before he had time to hear of his former patron's satisfaction, he was already on his way to Leipzig. There he remained for at least a couple of weeks, but there is no known record of his activities during that time. At the end of May or early in June he arrived at Berlin, most probably carrying letters from van Swietens. He played repeatedly for the King and his nephew, Louis Ferdinand, himself an experienced musician. When the court departed for one of the spas, it appears that Beethoven did not reply to an invitation from the King to accompany them—although it is not known whether this was in fact a contract or simply an ordinary invitation. Yet he still found the time to perform twice in the "Davidiana," Fasch's academy of singing, where he improvised on themes sung by the pupils. It was on one of these occasions that he met Zelter, as well as the director of court music, Himmel, though he apparently annoyed the two men by his "high tone." Of the return journey to Vienna nothing is known. It is probable that it was during this time that he was struck down by the "dangerous illness" which he had caught "through his own negligence." According to rather dubious sources he stopped off on the way at Prince Lobkowitz's house where he worked on the string quartets, and op. 18 was in fact dedicated to the Prince. The next verifiable date as to his movements is provided by an academy concert in Pressburg where he is reputed to have met his pupil, Countess Babette von Kegelvics, on November 23. To her he dedicated the *Grande Sonate* op. 7, known in Vienna as *The Beloved.*

Among the sketches dating from 1796 we find ideas for the septet, country dances, and bagatelles; for the scene *Ah perfido;* for the Quintet for Piano and Wind op. 16; for the Piano Sonata op. 7; for the six String Quartets op. 18; for songs such as "Der Kuss" ("The Kiss") and "Nahe des Geliebten" ("Close to the Beloved"). Likewise sketches for the revision of the Piano Concerto in B; for the "Opferlied" ("Song of Sacrifice"); the second of the Rondos for Piano in C major op. 51; and finally the setting for a song by Gellert known solely from its presence in his notebook. And all these ideas were simply jotted down in a fascinating whirl of inspiration. They are occasionally interspersed with words which are very important for the considerable light they throw on his process of composition. So for instance the words *"les derniers soupirs"* inserted to describe the end of the adagio of op. 18, no. 1:

op. 18, I

which was originally planned thus:

les derniers soupirs   Skizze

Beethoven had in fact given the first, greatly differing version of this quartet to his friend Amenda on the occasion of the latter's departure from Vienna in 1799. According to his own account, Beethoven played this slow quartet for him one day, asking for his impression and comments. Amenda apparently replied that it reminded him of the parting of two lovers, to which Beethoven is supposed to have said that he had imaged the scene to be taking place in the vault containing the tombs of Romeo and Juliet.

It is, of course, uncertain to what extent these reports can be considered reliable, but it does touch upon what is probably the most tricky question concerning Beethoven's creativity: the question of the interpretation of his instrumental music. Even the uninitiated hearer of a Haydn quartet, a Mozart symphony, or a Beethoven sonata will feel that these works do not consist merely of the arrangement of arbitrary notes producing complementary sounds. If the most verbally articulate of the arts, namely poetry, speaks not to man's intellect but to his capacity to feel, we can therefore say that all the arts, regardless of their greatly differing means of expression, manifest themselves according to the same structural laws. Observations such as those made by Goethe when confronted with the initially puzzling phenomenon of the Strassburg Cathedral can in essence be applied to all the arts: "A work of art, the whole of which is conceived in large, simple, harmonious parts, does indeed make a solemn and noble impression, but the real enjoyment produced by pleasure can come only from the harmony of all the fully developed individual elements" (*Poetry and Truth,* Book 9).

If we may apply in general terms a statement made in connection with Mozart, that "it is impossible to define great art by an analysis of its component parts" (Greither), then it is equally impossible to play off one great artist against another. Those who do not admire Haydn unreservedly, and cannot genuinely love Mozart's melodic language will be every bit as incapable of understanding Beethoven or of feeling the "god-like flashes" in Schubert. And yet these composers are really worlds apart; for where Haydn's music depicts the dignity of man, where Mozart's genius lay in his ability to depict human feelings and sentiments, and where Schubert was famed for the magical quality of his overwhelming melodies, Beethoven was considered right from the beginning as the "musician of ideas." This can be seen from his own admission that "even in my instrumental music I always have the work as a whole before my eyes." But just what is this whole, this entirety? Even his own contemporaries puzzled and hazarded guesses, trying to track down any statements which the composer might have concealed in his works. The most extensive studies of this kind were those made by Arnold Schering, who put forward intuitively deduced possible "poetic models" for over a third of all Beethoven's major works. The decisive factor was the temperament of the listener, and this determined what kind of "decoding system" he would need. If we can trust Schindler, Beethoven's last confidant—who also counted himself among those who relied on such explanations—it was Beethoven's own intention to unveil and elucidate his instrumental works. While he was undoubtedly inspired and excited by dramatic moments in the works of Homer, Shakespeare, and Schiller, which he was then able to translate into music, we are still bound by his own statement that "one leaves it to the listener to discover the situation . . . Even without a description one can recognize the whole, which is more a sensation than a symphony" (1807). Indeed, the most frequently quoted impression—especially of the symphonies and overtures—speaks in terms of a kind of "ethos-making power" (Georgiades), while others have experienced them as "forms made tangible," which fulfills Beethoven's own words when he spoke of "fashioning broadly and closely, high and low."

A short time later, in 1800, he sent the setting of "Adelaide" (composed five years previously) to the author of the original poem, Friedrich von Matthisson, together with the following words: "You yourself know what a difference a few years can bring for an artist who is continually progressing . . ." This illuminates precisely his lifelong striving to achieve the even greater "density" of his musical language and composition or, as he phrased it, "the isolation of the various voices." Due to certain overlaps of production it is not possible to determine any definite chronological order for his compositions, though we can refute the "three styles" thesis, for every subsequent work represents "experiment and perfection combined." Though his friends may have missed this, they must have noticed other changes. Thus we find the eldest von Breuning, who met Beethoven on his return from Berlin, writing to Wegeler: ". . . that through his travels he has become somewhat steadier, or rather he has become a better judge of human nature, convinced of the rarity and worth of true friends," which more or less reiterates the comment of the former court marshall that "he is said to have improved beyond measure." While the threat of a French invasion had caused Wegeler and the three von Breuning brothers to flee Bonn for Vienna, the warlike conditions in Italy also led the von Kügelgen brothers to leave Rome temporarily for the safety of Vienna. Their arrival there was followed by that of the two Rombergs with whom Bee-

thoven gave an academy concert in order to bolster their fi-
nances. This was the first occasion on which the Berlin sonatas
were heard in public in Vienna. The arrival of Bernadotte as
Napoleon's ambassador brought about his meeting with the
violinist Rodolphe Kreutzer, who belonged to the ambassador's
suite. Unfortunately, there are no details available, but it is
known that Beethoven was impressed by the "aggressive manner and technique" of the powerful circles around Cherubini
and Mehul. Presumably he also met Bernadotte himself. On the
other hand, the reports of piano competitions with the extremely
competent Joseph Wölffl and J. B. Cramer, whom Beethoven
himself esteemed greatly and who was one of the best pianists
in the entire continent, are all enveloped in anecdote. His friendship with the double-bass virtuoso Dragonetti also dates from
this time.

In spite of all this Beethoven still managed to conceal an
observation that had been troubling him for quite some time;
namely the onset of his deafness. Even his closest friends, Wegeler and Amenda, did not hear about it until three years later
in 1801, on the death of Lenz von Breuning, who had been
a particular favorite of Beethoven. And even then they were
charged to keep it a closely guarded secret, not to be entrusted
to anyone whatever. "Let me tell you that my most prized
possession, my hearing, has greatly deteriorated . . . That my
hearing will improve I must hope, it is true, but I hardly think
it possible, for diseases of this kind are the most difficult to
cure . . . Oh how happy should I be now if I had perfect hearing, for then I would join you immediately. But in my present
condition I must withdraw from everything. . . . Sad resigna-
tion." His ears, he said later, continued to buzz day and night,
sometimes reduced him to despair, and gave rise to eccentric
speculation and plans, even to thoughts of suicide. They became a permanent problem for him: ". . . in my profession it

49

is a terrible handicap." He skillfully succeeded in concealing the fact for quite a long time from Viennese society, though it was more than once attributed to his moodiness when he failed to answer a question. It would be only too understandable if this depression had had a derogatory effect on his creative ability. But the sequence of Beethoven's works does not, as has frequently been insinuated, reflect the chronological circumstances of his life in music. Besides, his periods of inspiration, mental assimilation, and actual composing continually overlapped, and the whole process of composing any one work sometimes lasted for years.

If we compare the structure of his first drafts with the final form of his works, we are struck by the astonishing simplicity of notation in the former. When Beethoven in later years once admitted that "one definitely writes better when one knows that one is writing for the public . . . just as when one writes rapidly," it is in fact to be understood as a kind of self-justification, in the same way that he always used the "rapid creation" of a composition as an excuse to his publishers. But the sketches afford us all the more insight into the other changes he effected; the final form often has little in common with the first arrangements, as can be seen clearly from a comparison of the plan and final version of the andante from op. 18 no. 5:

String quartet playing had been extremely popular in Vienna long before Beethoven ever came there. Strange as it may seem, its origins were unknown, but it is thought to go back to the "Sinfonia à Quatre" as it was still published by the Mannheim maestros Gossec and Wagenseil, *"pour la comodité des grands et petits concerts."* Nevertheless, Haydn's Quartet in B major composed in 1750 for a certain Baron von Fürnberg near Melk is considered to be the first example composed expressly for a string ensemble made up of soloists, as against the former "ad libitum" practice. It soon became the custom to bring out overtures and even entire operas "en quator," which on the one hand increased the popularity of the operas and on the other enriched the still slender supply of quartet music. Even Beethoven's *Fidelio* was published scored for the quartet by Simrock in 1814/15. Whereas the majority of earlier quartet compositions seem to prefer the pattern of the "quators concertants"

Ignaz Schuppanzigh. Portrait by Josef Danhauser.

51

in which the first violin always took the lead and almost always performed the more virtuoso parts alone, the "quators dialogues" type—as cultivated by the Mannheimers—incorporated a far greater participation on the part of the other instruments. There seem to have been various independent centers where the quartet was cultivated, though there can be no doubt that the Viennese, headed by Haydn and Mozart, eventually led the field.

In a little-known novel of 1865, *Das Quartett* by W. H. Riehl, is to be found the most faithful description of the intimate society as Beethoven encountered it with Lichnowsky and Rasumowsky and the circle of the Schuppanzigh quartet. A great many of Beethoven's first friends in Vienna were cellists—Zmeskall, Brunsvik, and Gleichenstein—but it was a Count Apponyi who actually commissioned the first quartet. He in fact never received it, for the first version for four parts was preceded by versions for three and five parts, due possibly to compositional speculation which he lacked the experience to resolve. He is thought to have taken his problem to E. A. Förster, in whose honor the Schuppanzigh group met to play quartets twice a week. Being an expert composition teacher and a well-known composer of quartets, Förster was well able to acquaint Beethoven with the particular difficulties of composing for strings rather than for piano. Though Beethoven's first sketches for the famous six string quartets of op. 18 date from the period of his tuition under Albrechtsberger, he seems to have taken the work seriously only after the revision of the second piano concerto. Nevertheless, the first draft of op. 18 no. 1 (no. 3 having preceded it) was sent to Amenda on June 25, 1799. Two years later all six quartets had been published, in two parts, and dedicated not without reason to Prince Lobkowitz. Since public quartet concerts did not draw such large crowds as did academy concerts, it was all the easier to find a suitable hall in which to hold them, although we also know that concerts were staged on occasion in the unusual setting of the cafés of the Augarten and the Prater, where Schuppanzigh in some years even organized subscription concerts. It is not generally known that immediately afterwards Beethoven himself transcribed his Piano Sonata op. 14 no. 1 for strings. As he informed his publisher: ". . . and I know that no one else could do this as easily." As is known, he had transcribed a quartet by Haydn long before, and it cannot be ruled out that it was the "Old Master" of quartet composition who possibly gave Beethoven the initial impetus to write four-part string compositions. By the next quartet compositions he had begun to grant equal rights to all four instruments, and to give more weight to the middle parts, to which the fugues and polyphonic approach of his famous predecessors seemed to lend themselves particularly well.

The most contradictory accounts of his personal appearance at this time have come down to us—ranging from "the perfect cavalier" to "the image of Robinson Crusoe." Since portrait painters obviously treated dress in the most conventional manner, and since most descriptions concerning his appearance date from the last years of his life, neither can really be regarded as fully reliable and trustworthy. If we are to believe that he was often awkward and erratic in his movements, that he was disfigured by pock marks, and that he was absolutely helpless and unteachable in anything to do with either household or money matters, it must have been solely the fascination of his inspired playing that literally tore down all class barriers and opened all doors to him with friendships of the most intimate nature. As Wegeler wrote: "In Vienna, at least for as long as I was living there, Beethoven was always involved in romantic affairs, including not a few conquests which many an Adonis would have found, if not impossible, at any rate extremely difficult." But this had already been the case in Bonn, where he had worshipped first of all a girl called Jeanette von Honrath, then his pupils Baroness von Westerholt and Eleonore von Breuning, and probably also the pretty Babette Koch from the "Zehrgarten" circle who later married into the Belderbusch family.

It is significant that he always maintained the utmost discretion, never disclosed a name, and was extremely cautious with letters, so that the identity of the women with whom he was involved can be based only on supposition, or, to be more precise, on a mixture of suspicion, coincidence, anecdote, and desire for self-importance on the part of the person who supplied the information. The comment in a letter to Simrock: "Are your daughters grown up yet? Train one of them to be my bride!" bears the unmistakable stamp of Beethoven's sense of humor. Yet the claim that he proposed marriage in Vienna to a singer, Magdalene Willmann, whom he had already met back in Bonn, is based solely on a statement made all of sixty years later by her stepsister, who gave as the reason for the refusal: "Because he was so ugly and half mad." Magdalene, who continued to appear frequently at concerts with Beethoven even after her marriage to Galvani, died in 1801. From the same year dates a letter to Wegeler (November 16) in which Beethoven speaks of "a dear, enchanting girl" who has given him "for the first time the feeling that marriage might bring me happiness. Unfortunately, she is not of my class, and at present I could not marry her in any case—I still have to bustle around a good deal . . ." From his pupil Ries we hear the mysterious words to the effect that a certain, naturally unnamed lady "has captivated him most strongly of all, and longest too—for seven whole months." To the same period belongs his association with two young ladies of the Brunswick family, as well as their cousin Giulietta Guicciardi. It must be more than a coincidence that his relationship with each of these three women—and with many others in the years to come—seems to have aimed at translating sudden attraction into deep love, only to fade away each time to the accompaniment of depression and melancholy. Leaving aside the more personal aspects, we may well imagine that such symptoms were intimately connected with the rhythm of his creativity, and that his path was always to lead from the sensuous to the transcendental, from the perigee to the apogee, from eros to ethos. As he himself expressed it: "You may not be a person for your own benefit, only for that of others. For you there can be no happiness other than what you have in yourself, in your art . . ." We can thus picture his life as a continuous up and down, flowing and ebbing like the tide; receiving and giving, torn between the desire for the company of others and the equally driving need for solitude. This behavior must have seemed exceedingly odd, and no doubt caused him to be dismissed as a crank by many an unsuspecting observer. It demanded the complete subordination of everything else in his life, resulted in his often abruptly changing relationships with both patrons and friends, and dictated his attitude toward the affairs of his household and servants. And in addition it determined his outward appearance at any given time: elegant or neglected, out of his wits or wrapped in thought.

Since neither journeys nor any other external events were ever really important enough to become landmarks of the various stages of his life, the sole means we have of establishing the progress of his career is to be found in the "birthdates" of his works. Although further complicated by the fact that he had the habit of working on several different projects simultaneously, one can generally say that 1795 was the year of the Piano Trio, 1796 that of the String Quartet in E-flat, and 1797 the year of the *Grande Sonate* for Countess Kegelvics, for whom he doubtless had a passion at the time. 1798 is dominated by the *Sonate Pathetique,* while 1799 sees the composition of the

First Symphony and 1800 that of the Horn Sonata and the Septet—all embedded in a shower of "meteorites" of varying sizes.

I LIVE ONLY IN MY MUSIC

IN a letter to Friedrich von Matthisson, Beethoven himself refers to the shyness which he says prevented him from sending Matthisson earlier his setting of his poem "Adelaide," and one is tempted to suspect that some similar inhibitions must have held him back from composing his first symphony. His fame at this time was doubtless based above all on his large numbers of piano works: both press and public mentioned him in the same breath with Clementi, Cramer, Eberl, Wölffl, Steibelt, and Dussek. But even if we revere the most sublime revelations of Beethoven's art in the form of his last quartets, we cannot fail to see that the greatest and most powerful effect was released only in his symphonies.

When Maximilian Franz was reduced to a position in the Teutonic Order, he had had placed at his disposal by the Kaiser the small castle of Seilern not far from Schönbrunn, where he lived when not at Mergentheim. That Beethoven spent the following summer there (1801) cannot have been due to just a passing mood. After the first performance of the First Symphony in April 1800, the work was acquired by Hoffmeister for publication, and in June 1801 Beethoven supplied the following dedication text for the work: "*à son altesse serenissime Maximilian François.*" This was precisely at the time of the composer's stay with the Elector, who eventually died—after a long illness —at the end of the same month, apparently under Beethoven's very eyes. Whether a legacy for Beethoven was included in the will, or whether Lichnowsky's readiness to guarantee him 600 florins per annum in future "for as long as he does not find a suitable position" is connected with it, we do not know. Even if the dedication of the symphony was transferred to Baron van Swieten, the title page still bears the arms of the Elector. Beethoven's intention may in all probability be interpreted as his way of paying his last respects and as a proof of complete reconciliation.

Two years previously, in 1799, he had dedicated the two piano sonatas of his op. 14 to Baroness von Braun, and had thus unwittingly or deliberately gained himself an entry into the royal theaters, of which Baron von Braun was assistant manager. It was he who in April 1800 granted Beethoven permission to hold a concert in the Hofburg theater. This was the first concert Beethoven himself organized, and very soon there were clashes of opinion, as was almost inevitably the case throughout Beethoven's life. He wanted Wranitzky to conduct, while the Italian orchestra insisted on having their leader, Conti. Besides two excerpts from the *Creation* and a Mozart symphony, the program included the first performance of the First Symphony, the Septet, and a piano concerto, and in addition to this Beethoven then improvised freely on the piano. Allowance had not been made for sufficient rehearsals, which caused one critic to complain about the orchestra, and about the wind players in particular. But he nevertheless reached the conclusion that it was "the most interesting concert for a long time . . .," and mentions the "symphony, which contained a great deal of skill, novelty, and a wealth of ideas." In this symphony Beethoven established his standard complement—i.e., twice as many wind instruments as usual—but in relation to the small proportion of strings this created a top-heavy effect which he had not intended. It would be unfair to compare this symphony with his later works; it simply represented a closer connection with Haydn's late works than with Mozart, rich in technical details of instrumentation. In any event, it was acclaimed as a "faultless masterpiece," and it was clearly to be reckoned with that each and every subsequent symphony would depart more and more from convention, and bring out more and more of Beethoven's individuality. Shortly after this he wrote to Wegeler: "I live only in my music. I have barely finished one work before the next one is already begun. The way I write at the moment, I often produce three or four things at the same time" (June 29, 1801).

Shortly after this concert in the Hofburg theater, another concert took place featuring the most famous horn player of the time, Wenzel Stich, otherwise known as Punto. A Bohemian by birth, he was a natural talent—Mozart had already composed for him—who spent his time wandering restlessly between Paris and Prague, giving concerts as he went. Though Beethoven had already announced a new horn sonata, it was actually committed to paper only a short time before it was due to be performed. When Punto won an unexpectedly enthusiastic reception with this work, he persuaded his composer to accompany him to Budapest. This was preceded by a contest with Daniel Steibelt, an extremely prolific piano composer and erstwhile child prodigy who, however, had a tendency to charlatanism. The two encounters took place in the house of the fashionable banker, Count Fries, to whom Beethoven dedicated no fewer than four important works (including the Seventh Symphony). While Beethoven introduced himself to Steibelt with his masterly Clarinet Trio op. 11, a work which undoubtedly outweighed Steibelt's entire production, the latter demonstrated brilliantly in his latest "tremolo style" and made Beethoven amply aware of the condescension of a much-traveled and successful man. Eight days later, and in the meantime more informed about the value of Steibelt's arpeggios, Beethoven picked up the cello part of one of Steibelt's quintets, and beat out a theme from the upside-down score, which he distorted so cruelly that Steibelt left the room in a rage and shortly after departed from Vienna. Also on record are the concerts in May and June in honor of a certain Countess Pawlowna at which "Messrs. Bethorn [!] and Punto" participated. But when these were over, Beethoven was at long last able to surrender himself to the pleasures of the country in Unterdöbling, filling his sketchbooks with drafts for the Violin Sonatas (op. 23) and especially for the so-called *Spring Sonata,* op. 24. He also worked on the piano sonatas with the world-famous *marcia funebre* and the one *quasi una fantasia* (op. 27), as well as contributions for the Second Symphony; but his greatest efforts seem to have been devoted to the music for the ballet *Geschöpfen des Prometheus.* While his only publication in 1800 was a small series of variations all based on a single theme, the following year saw the publication of ten times the amount (chiefly by Mollo at Vienna); in fact almost all his works from op. 15 to op. 24, hence including the first two piano concertos, the quartets, and the First Symphony.

The idea of getting Beethoven to compose some ballet music for the Hofburg Theater is generally ascribed to the influence of the Empress, to whom Beethoven had dedicated the Septet. His manuscript remarks indicate how seriously he set to work and came to terms with the choreography and the stage directions for the dancers. It was a task which could not fail to stimulate his enthusiasm, because it involved him in "painting the fantastic effect" of his own art. Since his Viennese notebooks have not been preserved, the only part of Beethoven's music to have survived is the overture, which is similar in construction to the First Symphony. The sixty pages of sketches for the overture and the subsequent sixteen numbers bear witness to the pains Beethoven took over the composition. The echo of the contemporary press confirmed that only Neider could deny the absolutely perfect quality of his music, and even Haydn was prepared to offer some friendly compliments.

The busy year 1801 began with various concerts, and the months following the premiere of *Prometheus* in March found Beethoven once again involved in dealings with publishers. After this he seems to have had his attention drawn to the derogatory reviews of his most recent works, the first three violin sonatas and the variations, which had appeared in the *Allgemeine Musikalische Zeitung*: ". . . what bizarre, tiresome movement . . . devoid of method . . . a search for unusual modulation, a revulsion against normal combinations, so much so that one cannot but lose all patience with and pleasure in it . . . Whether he is as happy a composer as he is a skilled pianist is a question that—to judge by the rehearsals in question—is much more difficult to answer . . . such transitions are and remain flat . . ." It was not a reaction to the review, but to allusions made by Härtel in a letter, when Beethoven then wrote to his publishers: "Advise your reviewers to show a little more caution and intelligence, especially with regard to the productions of young composers . . . I should never have mentioned a syllable of this if you yourself had not raised the point." His friend Hoffmeister was informed even more equivocally: "As for the Leipzig reviewers, just let them talk. They will certainly never make anyone immortal with their chatter, nor will they ever take immortality from anyone upon whom Apollo has bestowed it."

Hand in hand with the haggling that went on concerning the distribution of his works, which he felt to be unworthy, the miseries of his domestic situation increased when he gave up his rooms at Prince Lichnowsky's on account of the unbearable social duties he was called upon to undertake while living

Ferdinand Ries.

there. His inability to deal with servants and landlords or to make ends meet with the means at his disposal doubtlessly robbed him of many a precious hour. It must in all justice be mentioned that he was never without some helpful soul prepared to support him in need. At this point that role was taken up by his brother Karl, and his pupil Ries, whom he assured in return: "None of my friends shall ever be wanting so long as I still have a penny to my name."

The extent to which he had by then become a focus of public interest can be seen from Kotzebue's journal, *Der Freimüthige,* where the differing reactions of the public when confronted with any new work of Beethoven are extremely well described: in the first instance those particular admirers who joyfully acclaimed anything from his pen; secondly, the

61

indecisive, who drew up short at the Septet and the First Symphony; and lastly the antagonists who rejected outright the "strange and fantastic" elements in Beethoven's music. It speaks for his self-confidence that he did not let himself be disconcerted by even the most adverse criticism: "Even if it comes like a flea bite, it is all over in a flash, and the minute the sting has gone the whole thing merely strikes me as a great joke." Despite his enemies—"of whom there are not a few"— he felt that "my physical energy and so too my intellectual strength have been increasing more than ever for some time now. With each day I come closer to my goal; I feel it, yet I cannot describe it." Due perhaps to that Flemish element of his ancestry, "clever and courageous, yet restless and voluptuous" and never content with whatever he had learned or attained, he was forever driven compulsively onward along his self-chosen path.

Although at times he himself said he "could not avoid some idleness," he undertook an immense number of works in the period 1800 to 1802. These included the piano sonata with the "fluttering" rondo for Count Browne; the "highly poetical" op. 26 with the funeral march for Lichnowsky; the two *quasi una fantasia* sonatas (op. 27) for two grand ladies—Princess J. Liechtenstein and his own Countess Giulietta Riccardi— without a doubt the crowning achievement of his entire compositions for the piano; the *grand sonate* for the old man who had once wanted Lessing to move to Vienna, an extremely headstrong work. Then there was the Sonata op. 31 which he himself described as a "novella cycle." They demand the utmost precision of the interpreter to bring out their true verve and vitality. All these creations say so much more about Beethoven than any number of letters can possibly do. As well as the two series of variations on original themes (op. 15 and op. 35) and the seven Bagatelles for Piano (op. 33), this period also saw the composition of the Third Piano Concerto, in Beethoven's all-powerful C minor, and with its three incomparably distinctive movements. And between all these works we find such fine compositions as the String Quintet in C major (op. 29) also unjustly known as the "disguised symphony": no less ingenious or self-confident, but with a slight hint of the concertante, and with an adagio scarcely equalled for its warmth, the personification of goodness that so often permeates Beethoven's music. Of the Second Symphony the only part that is usually remembered—apart from the well-known larghetto—is the finale with its irresistibly powerful metre. In the same period he also composed German dances by the bundle, the Romances in G major and F major (op. 40 and op. 50 respectively), the latter even more popular than the former, a handful of violin sonatas, again including one in C minor with its willful scherzo, and lastly the profound Sonata in G major, so rich in ideas, a true dialogue sonata full of wit and movement. The second of the two Rondos for Piano which constitute op. 51, self-contained, certainly not without a self-conscious mannerism which exploits the essence of the music to the limits: "God alone knows why my piano music should still make the worst impression on me, especially when it is badly played . . ." (1804). All in all, this was an output that showed him at the peak of his creativity, and only lack of time prevented him from doubling it. It took him almost ten years to submit the entire harvest to the publishers, so that not a month passed throughout the next few years without the publication of some new composition—not to mention the arrangements and new editions of earlier works. In contrast to this profusion it seems odd that none of the works of his contemporaries published at the same time has survived, though their motifs, formal construction, and instrumentation show definite technical skill.

Only towards the end of the summer vacation was it possible for him to assess the extraordinary amount of work he had produced during the year. In July he wrote: "I have many new things, just say what you want . . ." In view of this the reader is all the more shocked by the sighs of deep depression which find their expression in the *Heiligenstadt Testament*: "O my fellow men, who consider me to be or describe me as hostile, cantankerous or misanthropic, how greatly do you wrong me. For you do not know the secret reason why I appear to be thus . . . just consider the fact that I have been afflicted by an incurable condition for six years . . . that my hopes of being cured have all been dashed . . . Though endowed with a fiery, lively temperament . . . I was soon forced to seclude myself and live in solitude . . . Thus I take leave of you . . . the cherished hope I brought here with me that I would be cured at least to a certain extent . . . even that hope I must now abandon completely . . ." (October 6–10, 1802). This *Testament* was discovered among his papers only after his death, and its authenticity is disputed because of the fact that the name of the composer's younger brother has been erased by an un-

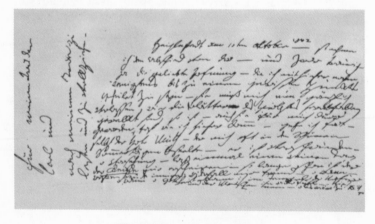

The Heiligenstadt Testament.

known hand. It was probably the outcome of his recognition that all attempts to restore his hearing had been in vain, which dawned on him fully when he noticed that he was unable to perceive sounds that his pupil Ries, who was accompanying him on a walk, was able to hear quite distinctly. In addition, the *Testament* was preceded by a period of overwork in self-imposed isolation. It was not until four years later that he forced himself to the decision not to conceal his deafness any longer, even with regard to his music. His next composition, the Second Symphony, the chief work of this phase, storms with the resolution "to seize fate by the throat." It is one of the "given facts" of his life that he virtually insisted on maintaining his solitude. As he wrote to Ries before the latter joined him in Heiligenstadt: "Don't bother to come here, because I have no time to waste."

If it is true that he turned up in Pistyan in Hungary that same year, it was probably there that he met Countess Erdödy, an excellent pianist, who had suffered an illness when very young and was partially lamed. The two were to be bound by the closest and warmest friendship for the rest of their lives, even when she was temporarily forced to leave the country through various obscure machinations. The artistic emancipation which came to complete fruition in his freely chosen creative medium of music now also began to make itself felt in his use of language. His letters became increasingly plastic in quality and show an inherent feeling for words that make it easy to imagine how enjoyable and sought-after his similarly erratic conversation must have been. The previous year he had informed Wegeler in a letter whose "composition" would do honor to any symphonic arrangement, that his financial position "was not bad," that his works brought in a substantial income and that he had more commissions than he could possibly cope with. When Hoffmeister sent him the commission for a sonata

Heiligenstadt, Probusgasse 6.

for an unknown lady, he hissed back: "Has the devil got hold of you all, gentlemen, that you suggest that I should write such a sonata? Well, perhaps at the time of the revolutionary fever such a thing might have been possible, but now, when everything is trying to slip back into the old routine, now that Bonaparte has concluded his Concordat with the Pope—to write a sonata like that? Now, if it were a *missa pro Sancta Maria a tre voci* . . . I would take up my paint brush instantly and write off a *credo in unum* in one sweep with large pound notes. But, good heavens, such a sonata—in these newly begun Christian times—ho ho! There you must leave me out, you won't get anything from me." Nevertheless he declared that he was prepared to follow the lady's plan "from an aesthetic point of view." He then laid down his conditions for undertaking the commission: namely, that for a stipulated fee she would be entitled to keep the sonata for her exclusive use for one year, after which time he would have the right to publish it. "If she thinks it will do her any honor, she can ask me to dedicate the sonata to her."

He immediately found a reason for getting irritated about publishing practices, for the string quintet he had sold to Count Fries the previous year had been offered by his brother on his behalf to both Hoffmeister and Härtel. In March 1802 Härtel acquired it for thirty-eight ducats; printing and proof correction lasted until November. In the meantime, while Beethoven was in Heiligenstadt, it must have been performed frequently at the Count's house. Artaria in all probability heard it praised, and the violinist Conti must have given him a copy of the music with the permission of the owner, Count Fries. The latter, who was aware of Artaria's intention to publish the sonata, merely stipulated that Artaria could not put it up for sale until the Leipzig edition had been on offer in Vienna for at least two weeks. The Viennese publisher, believing he had the agreement of the owner, then sent Beethoven the copy to be used for printing, together with a request that he should check it for any possible errors of transcription. Only in this way did Beethoven come to hear of the matter and was doubtless unjustifiably so infuriated by the "villainy of that arch-rogue Artaria" that he instantly informed Härtel about it, in order to prevent the latter from suspecting that he himself had offered the work to Artaria. Further still, he returned the manuscript uncorrected to the Viennese publisher, though this did not stop him from publicly decrying the edition on its publication as being "full of mistakes, incorrect, and unusable for any pianist." Ries even claimed that Beethoven had given him the responsibility of having the copies received from Artaria "corrected" in such a way that they could not be sold. As can be seen from official records, the affair had to be brought to the attention of the

67

Chief of Police no fewer than ten times in the course of the following three years, and it can be well imagined that the unresolved conflict made any future cooperation with the most important publisher in the city out of the question for a good many years to come. This instance serves to illustrate the extremely dubious legal situation which existed at the time in the publishing world, a situation fostered by the contemporary political unheaval and unrest. For this reason it is understandable that Beethoven adopted the practice of having his works published if possible in Vienna, Leipzig, Paris, and London simultaneously, even to the point of fixing the same date of publication in all four cities. However, the continual negotiations imposed a heavy burden on him, which he detested beyond measure. (As is commonly known, not until two years after his death was a settlement reached establishing copyright and only ten years later still the ban on all illegal reproduction or reprints.)

In the winter of 1802/3 Beethoven returned in good time to Vienna, where he found temporary accommodation in the house of the "old maestro," E. A. Förster, whose son could still recollect years later the "painful" piano lessons he had had with Beethoven. From there he moved in with Stephan von Breuning who was just then in the throes of organizing another concert of Beethoven's works. As on previous occasions, it proved to be a monster program, including the First and Second Symphonies and the Piano Concerto in C minor, as well as the rapidly composed oratorio *Christus am Ölberg* (*Christ on the Mount of Olives*), set to a text by the librettist, Franz Xaver Huber. This now forgotten work for three solo voices, chorus, and orchestra was undoubtedly created—like the Lenten oratorios—to furnish the "theaterless" days with some ecclesiastical material. The concert on April 5, 1803 was preceded by a rehearsal that lasted from eight in the morning until half-past two in the afternoon.

Prince Lichnowsky had thoughtfully provided the large audience with sandwiches, meat, and wine so as to persuade them to stay for the repetition of the oratorio. Even so the length of the program (which had already been shortened as it was), weighed heavily against the success of the concert. Once again, all renderings clearly suffered from insufficient preparation, even the piano concerto, and it is thus astonishing that one critic should have acknowledged that "Beethoven in time will be able to effect a revolution in music just as Mozart did. He is already moving with large strides towards this goal." Through the Schuppanzigh circle Beethoven was introduced a month later to George Bridgetower, the mulatto violinist in the service of the Prince of Wales, and participated in a concert with him in the Augarten that May. He then composed for Bridgetower the Violin Sonata op. 47, also known as the *Kreutzer* Sonata because he is reputed to have taken as his motif a theme originat-

The "Avenue of Sighs" in the Augarten, Vienna.

ing from Kreutzer—possibly from his nineteenth Violin Concerto.

The first performance is said to have aroused nothing but derision. That Bridgetower—with whom Beethoven allegedly fell out over a girl—was an outstanding violinist is evident from the way his improvisation of certain passages in the concerto caused Beethoven to leap to his feet, embrace him, and exclaim: "Again, again, my dear fellow." At the same time the Schuppanzigh circle began rehearsing the piano sonatas which had been rescored for string quartet. During Beethoven's lifetime even the *Pathétique* (op. 13) was partially transcribed for wind quartet, string quartet and for the piano (four hands).

Schikaneder must in the meantime have chosen an opportune moment to start negotiations with Beethoven in the hopes of persuading him to compose an opera score. There was certainly no dearth of competent composers available in Vienna at the time, but the public had become dissatisfied, and the feeling was that German opera was being pushed more and more into the

Theater an der Wien. Contemporary engraving.

background. Both the court theaters still stood at the time under the direction of Baron Braun. In the course of just over a year Schikaneder's theater had become "the most splendid theater in Germany," thanks to the financial backing of the businessman Zitterbarth. Gleaming in blue and silver, its two floors and five tiers of boxes could accommodate six thousand people, and its elliptical design and the unusual width of its stage were particularly noted. Admittedly, the first play staged there was a failure, but the three Cherubini operas that followed caused a far greater sensation than the plays put on by Braun. Rivalry reached a climax when Mehul's *Wagen gewinnt* (*He who dares, wins*) was staged at both theaters simultaneously. While Braun went off to Paris to engage Cherubini's services for his theaters, Schikaneder gave Abbé Vogler—the teacher of Carl Maria von Weber and Meyerbeer—commissions for three operas, at the same time submitting to Beethoven the libretto for *Vesta's Fire* that he himself had either composed or adapted. By the time Vogler had produced his first opera, *Samori,* Beethoven had only completed four passages of his. Then in April 1804 Zitterbarth sold the theater secretly to Baron Braun. Schikaneder was immediately dismissed and replaced as director by Joseph von Sonnleithner. It was he who tracked down Bouilly's libretto for *Léonore ou l'amour conjugal,* out of which was to grow Beethoven's *Fidelio.*

WITHOUT WISHING TO SET MYSELF UP AS AN EXAMPLE...

As early as the summer of 1803, while he was working on his preparations for *Vesta's Fire* in Baden and Oberdöbling, he was already preoccupied with another project far more suited to him, his Third Symphony, "in homage to Napoleon" as he wrote in his own hand on one of the copies that have come down to us intact. It was on the merits of this work that the masses were to judge him as a composer: "Beethoven has reproduced in music the worldwide storm of revolution; fearful and yet wholly

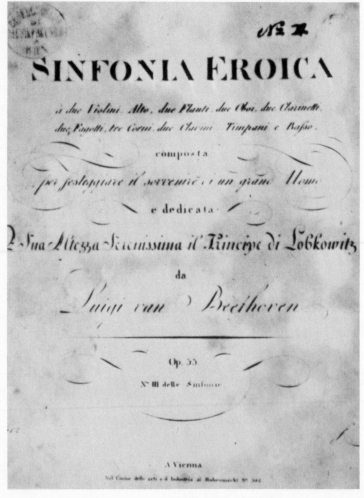

Frontispiece of the Symphony no. 3 (*Eroica*).

captivated we follow him with our ear as he hovers at the boundaries of harmony with such well-timed audacity. What is possibly his most glorious allegro bore Napoleon's name until Beethoven became furious at the Consul having himself proclaimed emperor" (L. Bauer, 1839). When the symphony was eventually published in October 1806 it was dedicated merely "to the memory of a great man." No other symphony of Beethoven's caused such a stir as this *Eroica,* which so clearly breaks new ground and, without ever attempting to "paint," nevertheless gives definite expression to heroism.

During this restless period of dubious political intrigues, when the greater part of the support for Napoleon stemmed in reality from the increasing antipathy towards the petty tyranny of both

Archduke Rudolf of Austria.

73

the secular and ecclesiastical systems, Beethoven was fated for a renewed link with the House of Hapsburg. The Archduke Rudolf, a nephew of the Elector Max Franz and stepbrother of the Emperor, probably met Beethoven for the first time in the Elector's salon and certainly felt the most sincere admiration for him. He then became Beethoven's pupil, and in later years became the only person to be instructed by him in the art of composition. According to Schindler the piano part of the Triple Concerto op. 56, which dates from the same time as the *Eroica* and the *Leonora* overtures, was written to accommodate the technical ability of Beethoven's royal pupil. Be that as it may, the Fourth Piano Concerto of two years later was in fact the first work expressly dedicated to Rudolf. It was the first of an impressive series of such dedications. In the Archduke Beethoven also gained a protector upon whom he remained dependent—to an extent that could easily seem exaggerated—for the rest of his life. Even apart from the aspect of financial assistance, Beethoven unquestionably owed the Archduke a great deal more than what we actually have on record. During the last ten years of his life, when he no longer made any secret of his contempt for "the aristocratic vermin," he still made an emphatic exception of archdukes—in particular his pupil—regardless of how trying the often excessive and inconvenient demands of royal service must at times have been to him.

Despite steadily increasing difficulties with his hearing Beethoven continued to frequent the salons of Viennese high society. He appeared at both morning and evening engagements, frequently participating in performances, and, when in the mood, even improvising, much to the delight of the entire company. Unfortunately, all accounts of these occasions are without exception littered with anecdotes, exaggerations, and generalizations. Hence, for instance, the story concerning the attempt to reproduce the "divine length" of the *Eroica* when, at a concert staged by the Lobkowitz orchestra in Vienna, Prince Louis Ferdinand is reputed to have been so fascinated by the work that

Portrait by Willibrord Mähler, 1804.

it was then repeated a second and even a third time. On other occasions he is said to have knocked over a table piled with china; to have hit in the face the boy carrying a chandelier for him so that it was smashed to pieces; and to treat his piano in such a way that with each chord he had the strings jumping by the dozen. There may well be a grain of truth in all these anecdotes, but in the form that they have been handed down to us not one of them is really credible. People must literally have lain in wait in the hopes of witnessing his supposed capriciousness without ever realizing that he had become more than simply one of Vienna's "characters."

One is tempted to consult the portraits of Beethoven executed at this time—the painting by Stainhauser that unfortunately we know only through prints, the miniature by Christian Hornemann, and Mähler's portrait with the upheld hand—but they produce no one conclusive answer. There are astonishingly few verbal descriptions of him in these years. "He is," wrote a young Englishman who saw him conduct *Fidelio* in 1805, "a small, dark man, still quite youthful-looking, and he wears glasses . . ." Ignaz von Seyfried, the musical director of the Schikaneder Theater, gave the following frank account of his impressions at the end of the competition with Wölffl: "Even at that stage, Beethoven in no way tried to conceal his temperamental inclination to the sinister and gloomy when improvising. As soon as he submerged himself in the infinite realm of music he was lost to the world. Intellect had shattered all restrictive fetters, shaken off the yoke of servitude and flown off with victorious jubilations into shining infinities . . ." The *Leipzig Music Magazine* said that Beethoven "played extremely brilliantly, though not very delicately, and he sometimes drifts into obscurity. He appears to the greatest advantage in his free improvisations. Especially there, it is quite extraordinary with what lightness of touch and yet with what firmness in his sequence of ideas

Beethoven takes a theme and does not simply vary the phrases —the delight, and pride, of many a virtuoso—but carries it right on through to the end. Since the death of Mozart, who is still for me the non plus ultra, I have not found this kind of pleasure anywhere to the extent that I have experienced it in Beethoven's music."

At this time Beethoven is supposed to have admitted to his friend, the violinist Krumpholz, that he was no longer satisfied with his previous works, and that he wanted to take a different path. This "new path," whose outlines are already evident in the "quasi una fantasia" sonatas of op. 27, was to free him from the rigidity of what he termed "the musical skeleton," the doctrine of the appoggiatura. In this Beethoven was consciously distancing himself from the basic precepts of the Viennese school. He was not concerned with distinctions between "homophones" or "polyphones," sonatas or fugues, but rather with the correspondence between idea, form, and expression—the fundamental problem of all art forms. The "new" pieces which follow all differ from the "beautiful" tried-and-true ones—faultless, technically skilled, joyfully melodious and full of ideas— through their obvious plasticity and clarity of form, their richness of ideas, and their ponderousness. He may, of course, have found it almost unbearably restricting to have to take into consideration the inevitable "exposition, realization, and reprise" formula, though he never in fact dispensed with it even in his later works, as we can see by comparing the first movements of op. 18 no. 1, op. 59 no. 1, and op. 127. His intention of "isolating" the individual instruments can even be detected in the form, insofar as the secondary thoughts are expanded into complete episodes without succumbing to the romantic principle of "free, unrestrained fantasy." Though the "sublime length" is doubtless calculated to conceal the compositional form, it is nevertheless formal arguments that lead to expansion.

At precisely this moment Beethoven undertook a commission to compose an opera, and it was only much later that he realized "the concept of the whole," which he had always had "before the eyes" was now "broken into parts in a way." If his most original achievement had been that he succeeded in making the sayable unsayable—indeed to make it more sublime—he now had to think along completely different lines, bound to the spoken word and the vocal range and tone of the human voice. With respect to opera composing, it is conspicuous that Mozart virtually had no relationship to literature, while Beethoven, for whom "no treatise was too learned," was more at home with literature than any previous musician. Perhaps this accounts for his lifelong, futile search for a suitable libretto. Fortunately for him, Bouilly's book of the Leonora legend was simply played into his hands. By reason of its subject matter, based as it is on an incident personally experienced by the author, it was originally allotted to the dubious genre of the "horror-opera" as was the case with the versions by Gaveaux and the greatly underrated Paër. In Beethoven's hands, however, it is transformed into an almost symphonic opera. The dramatic nature of its theme meant that it was practically bound to be a success.

It was to be expected that Beethoven could not possibly follow the kind of methods of composition that enabled various of his contemporaries to turn out two hundred or more operas. Nevertheless, finding himself forced to take on several works simultaneously, he apparently singled out first of all the duet "Um in der Ehe froh zu leben" by way of a focal point, and placed it just before the finale to the first act. Mingled with ideas for Tiedge's poem "An die Hoffnung," the F minor Piano Sonata, a never-performed march and two movements from the Triple Concerto, we then find sketches for the first aria of the second act, the Quartet in D major, and Marzelline's aria.

K. auch k. k. pr. Schauspielh. a. d. Wien

NEUE OPER.

Heute Mittwoch den 20. November 1805
wird in dem k. auch k. k. priv. Schauspielhaus an der Wien
gegeben:

Zum Erstenmal:

FIDELIO,

oder:

Die eheliche Liebe.

Eine Oper in 3 Akten, frey nach dem Französischen bearbeitet
von Joseph Sonnleithner.

Die Musik ist von LUDWIG VAN BEETHOVEN.

Personen:

Don Fernando, Minister	Hr. Weinkopf.
Don Pizarro, Gouverneur eines Staatsgefängnisses	Hr. Meier.
Florestan, ein Gefangener	Hr. Demmer.
Leonore, seine Gemahlinn unter dem Namen Fidelio	Dlle. Milder.
Rocco, Kerkermeister	Hr. Rothe.
Marzelline, seine Tochter	Dlle. Müller.
Jaquino, Pförtner	Hr. Cache.
Wachehauptmann	Hr. Meister.
Gefangene.	

Wache. Volk.

Die Handlung geht in einem Spanischen Staatsgefängnisse einige Meilen von Sevilla vor.

Die Bücher sind an der Kassa für 15 kr. zu haben.

Preise der Plätze:

	fl.	kr.
Grosse Loge	10	—
Kleine Loge	4	30
Erstes Parterre und erste Gallerie	—	42
Erster Parterre und erste Gallerie ein gesperrter Sitz	—	56
Zweite Gallerie	—	30
Zweite Gallerie ein gesperrter Sitz	—	42
Zweites Parterre und dritte Gallerie	—	24
Vierte Gallerie	—	12

Die Logen und gesperrten Sitze sind bey dem Kassier des
k. auch k. k. National-Theaters zu haben.

Der Anfang um halb 7 Uhr.

Playbill for the first performance of *Fidelio* in 1805.

These are followed by some purely instrumental working ideas, as well as by some preliminary sketches for Rocco's so-called "golden aria," the duet from the second act, the last finale, a reworking of Leonore's first aria, notes for the first overture, and lastly some other sketches that do not belong to the opera at all. The sketch book gives the same impression as all his others; it is as if one inspiration produces its counterpart, as if he wanted to single out various qualities which should not impinge upon one another, as if he is balancing off the relative weights of different categories.

The "woeful story" of the various performances is all too familiar: the unfavorable circumstances of the moment in 1805 when the stalls were filled with French officers because the entire court, aristocracy, and all of Beethoven's friends had fled from

Prince Josef Franz Max Lobkowitz, 1799.

Vienna; and the criticism of those impatient listeners who were probably expecting to be regaled with some enchanting spectacle in the Viennese "sing and jingle" style. After just three performances the opera had to be withdrawn.

Convinced of its high creative value, and in order to prevent its being doomed to failure as an alleged "monstrosity," some of Beethoven's friends banded together to see if they could make the development of the plot more coherent. The ensuing second version, which was staged a year later, amounted to nothing but a "negative improvement," and when Beethoven then took it into his head that he was being swindled over the whole business, he withdrew his new score after just the second performance. On the occasion of its revival eight years later—it had been revised once more—the applause "exceeded all expectations." Freed from the confines of its imprisonment, the "story" had been transformed into a tale of unsurpassing claim, speaking not through words but through its music. It was a "consecration play" raised to the highest level of human experience.

Despite the humiliating experiences of 1805, Beethoven was enthusiastic about the genre, as can be seen from an entry among the sketches for op. 59, which also stands as a proof of his unshaken self-confidence. "Just as I plunged into the maelstrom of Viennese society, so too it must be possible to write operas in spite of all hindrances." Yet he also found "the whole business with the opera the most tiresome thing in the world" and a secret uneasiness seems to be contained in the resolution to "go back to my own ways." However, after the second *Fidelio* rehearsal in December, when there was a change of management in the theater and Baron Braun was replaced by a committee headed by Lobkowitz, Schwarzenberg, and Esterházy, Beethoven took courage again and volunteered to "compose at least one major opera annually as well as a small operetta or divertissement, and choruses or incidental pieces as they should be required or demanded." For this he was to receive a fixed salary of 2,400 ducats, all the takings from the third performance and a concert of his own works to be given for his benefit. The reasons he gives for his proposal are in themselves significant: that although he had to a certain extent won the favor and approval of aristocracy and general public alike, he had not as yet had the fortune to establish himself in Vienna in such a way that he could live totally for his art, and develop his talents to even greater perfection as he wished to do, ". . . to secure myself an independent future out of what until now have been merely chance advantages." The man in charge of court music, Count Dietrichstein, a declared disciple of Beethoven, found himself unable to accept the proposal, but was loath to have to pass on the information "for fear of making an unfavorable impression on a man he admired so greatly." By way of consolation, Beethoven was commissioned to write a mass for the Emperor, but "not too long or heavy . . . a mass for all, with only small solo parts. His Majesty loves fugues very much, when suitably executed, but not too long; the Sanctus and the Hosanna should be as brief as possible . . . and the Dona nobis pacem . . . without much cadence." After an enthusiastic beginning, work on the mass finally came to a standstill and it subsequently slipped into total obscurity.

This abortive attempt had been preceded by a visit to Prince Lichnowsky in Silesia, which had come to an abrupt end when Beethoven refused point blank to play before some French officers invited by the Prince. He is even alleged to have fled in the night to avoid the threat of house arrest. On reaching his own house, he is said to have smashed his bust of the Prince and to have written the following words to his Maecenas of so many years' standing: "Prince, what you are, you are through chance and birth; what I am, I am through my own merits . . ." Though no such letter has in fact come down to us, it is noticeable that from this time on no further dedication is made to Prince Lichnowsky, and all reports of the subsequent relations between the two men are of dubious authenticity. Two years after the break with Lichnowsky Beethoven wrote to the latter's neighbor in Silesia, Count Oppersdorf, to whom the Fourth Symphony is dedicated: "Things are improving for me . . . I have no need for people who want to torture their friends." This would seem to confirm the permanent estrangement of the two men. It probably also brought to an end the Prince's allowance to Beethoven. His next dedications went to Prince Lobkowitz and Count Rasumowsky, to Brunswick, Gleichenstein, and Countess Erdödy.

In 1804 Beethoven moved into the apartment found for him in the house on the Mölker Bastei belonging to Baron Pasqualati,

The Pasqualati house on the Mölker Bastei.

to which he then returned repeatedly in the course of the next decade. Today it is preserved as a memorial to the composer, and the visitor still goes up to his rooms by the same old, worn spiral staircase. Here it has somehow been possible to retain a trace of the atmosphere we associate with places directly connected with Beethoven such as Baden, Döbling, Hetzendorf, and Heiligenstadt, where he used to spend the summer months. Even today, these places help us to understand Beethoven's feeling of well-being when in the countryside. In May 1806 he was to have been accompanied to the country by his brother, but this plan was cancelled because of the latter's marriage to Johanna Reiss, the daughter of a well-to-do interior decorator. That September saw the birth of their son Karl, who was to cause his uncle more worry and trouble than all the irritations he ever encountered with concert arrangements and publishers. Some dishonesty on the part of his new sister-in-law seems to have led to a rift between the brothers, as a result of which Beethoven's "secretarial duties" were taken over by a colleague of von Breuning, the young Baron von Gleichenstein. Beethoven had just come to an agreement with the Scottish publisher, George Thomson, according to which he was to set to music various old English melodies—a commission that promised a welcome source of income for a good number of years. The following spring (1807) the usual academy concert was replaced by a subscription concert held at Prince Lobkowitz's house, at which the new Fourth Symphony, the Fourth Piano Concerto, and the *Coriolan* Overture were performed for the first time. Just a month later the possibility presented itself of drawing up an advantageous contract with Muzio Clementi concerning the circulation of his works in England.

It seems hardly to matter that works with which we must be very familiar if we are to understand them at all were greeted at their first performance with pomposity and prejudice: ". . . unworthy mystification . . . musical madness . . . insane . . . lunatic's patchwork . . ." On the other hand, of course, there was no dearth of intelligent and admiring enthusiasts. Clearly, such melodious works as the Violin Concerto and the *Coriolan* Overture were easier to appreciate than, for instance, the Fourth Symphony or the quartets. His motto: "I do not write for the gallery" was interpreted as if he composed specifically for the élite, though in fact he was concerned all his life with the "interests of the arts and the improvement of taste."

The period between 1806 and 1808 produced a diverse series of works of differing quality. The most important are those which bear the opus numbers 53 through 62 inclusive. Foremost among these is the *Waldstein* Sonata, the first "heavy" one, which is "self-contained" and requires no "imaginative powers"; and then the intellectually startling one that follows, so full of

First page of the Sonta for Pianoforte op. 57 (*Appassionata*).

contrast. This period includes the *Eroica,* the Triple Concerto, and the *Appassionata,* eruptive as almost no other piano poem, and marked with the puzzling designation "Fifty-first Sonata." Then there are the works addressed to quite a different audience; the Fourth Piano Concerto, with its powerfully swelling rondo, and the great quartets for Rasumowsky, technically demanding, intoxicating and unsurpassably mature throughout.

Also in the same group of works belongs the "eccentric" Fourth Symphony, the similarly melodious Violin Concerto—the apotheosis of its genre—and lastly the *Coriolan* Overture, which attempts to paint not events but sensations, and which has become the prototype of the classical overture.

The misery of his wordly life seemed to be firmly rooted in Beethoven's destiny as an integral counterpart to his rich inventiveness. Once the management of the theater decided to take up his offer, Lichnowsky's aid had come to an end, and concerts failed to produce any income to speak of—due to the extremely high overhead—Beethoven's sole source of income, since he was too proud to accept payment for either piano tuition or dedications, was from royalties. Following the disagreement with Artaria his compositions appeared with a number of different publishers, including Hoffmeister & Kühnel in Leipzig, and the firms of Löschenkohl, Mollo, and Cappi in Vienna. New connections, such as that with Pleyel in Paris, always seemed to offer more hope than actual success. Nevertheless, there had been an upswing in public opinion, and accusations such as: "exaggerated mannerism" or "affectedly complicated and difficult to perform" were few and far between. However, apart from one mass for Prince Esterházy (op. 86), he had received no commissions for some time either from a publisher, theater or concert impressario, or even from a wealthy prince, which meant that all initiative for planning had to come from him. Despite terrible headaches, he still managed to fill his sketchbooks with extensive ideas during his stay in the country—first in Baden, and then in Heiligen-stadt.

But he was then reminded that the mass had to take precedence, as it was due to be performed for the Princess's name-day that September. Legend has it that the Prince attacked Beethoven with the words: "But, my dear Beethoven, what have you been getting up to this time?" as a result of which Beethoven is supposed to have departed on the spot. But it cannot be untrue when the composer speaks to his publisher of the "great applause" that

Pencil sketch by Schnorr von Carolsfeld, around 1808.

he had received in Eisenstadt, adding that he felt he had handled the text in a way that had scarcely been touched on before. A highly personal kind of piety rises from each note, and it is significant that he recommended that it should be given its first performance in a concert hall, for which reason he wanted a German text to be set to it as well. While the copy handed over in Eisenstadt bore a handwritten dedication to the Prince, he must have had his reasons for dedicating the first printed edition of the mass first to Zmeskall, subsequently to "a young lady," and finally—the lady having married in the interim—to Prince Kinsky. Five years after the first performance the mass was published by Breitkopf & Härtel, just a few days before the Prince's fatal riding accident.

In the spring of 1808 a fingernail infection made it impossible for him to play himself, but Beethoven nevertheless appeared among the well-wishers who assembled to celebrate Haydn's seventieth birthday with a concert in his honor. In the meantime Beethoven had entered a condition of complete freedom—the very freedom he so longed for—which paradoxically made him incapable of reaching any decision at all. In the course of his long, wearisome search for suitable material for an opera he considered *Macbeth, Faust,* and *Bradamante.* By the end of the year he had turned his attention to the Indian operettas suggested by an Oriental specialist, and a book of oratorios entitled *The Deluge.* His notebooks contain notes and odd ideas connected with one or another of these projects. Another pair of symphonies also took final form at this time. The Fifth was completed in the spring of 1808, while the Sixth was composed at Heiligenstadt. They were both performed for the first time in December of that year at a concert which also contained excerpts from the Esterházy mass presented as hymns, an aria composed in Prague entitled *Ah perfido,* and the Fourth Piano Concerto. And as if that was not enough, in the last few weeks before the

concert was held he added the Choral Fantasy, the "Little Ninth."
Incidental friction led to the engagement of an inexperienced
singer instead of Anna Milder, and inadequate rehearsals had
such a derogatory effect on the vocal parts that one member of
the audience, Reichardt, wished that "he had had the courage to
leave sooner"—and this said of two symphonies which today are
among the best known and best loved of all. No detailed reports
about the concert have survived.

Though the concert itself brought in a certain profit and the
acceptance of the two symphonies, the mass, and other works by
Breitkopf & Härtel ensured still further revenue, he still found
himself forced to borrow money in order to pay a debt outstanding to his brother. Despite the fact that works of his were also
performed at other concerts, Beethoven himself must have been

Page from Beethoven's handwritten scores of the Sixth Symphony
(*Pastoral*).

all too aware of how remote his own situation was from the feeling of jubilation of the finale of the Fifth Symphony or from the "serene sensations" of merry togetherness and exultation evoked by the *Pastoral*. He must have realized that this was the price of independence in Vienna. Shortly before this he had received an offer from the King of Westphalia, Napoleon's youngest brother, Jérôme, to become director of court music in Cassel at a salary of six hundred gold ducats per annum—a sensation throughout the musical world. The summons had been conveyed by a German chamberlain and we can well imagine the horror of Beethoven's patrons—without exception loyal supporters of the Hapsburgs—when it became known that he was intending to accept the offer. Countess Erdödy was the first person to hear about these plans, and we can be quite sure that it was she who set to work to persuade Beethoven to stay in Vienna. She was soon followed by Gleichenstein and Zmeskall who were already busy working out practical suggestions. A "Plan for a Musical Institution" already made provision for a royal title for Beethoven, and Beethoven at his own request became a member of the theater committee with guaranteed regular concerts of his own works. Although on the one hand he wanted to avoid the appearance "that he was drawing a salary for nothing," he was practical enough to think of including a paragraph which was to commit even the heirs of his contract partners to continue payment. A draft in Gleichenstein's hand mentions Beethoven's "patriotic feeling towards his second fatherland," and speaks of the "distinguished and most highly esteemed personalities" who had urged Beethoven to make known the conditions under which he would consider staying in Vienna. These were eventually settled at four thousand ducats, and a contract to this effect was drawn up as early as February 26. According to this agreement Archduke Rudolf pledged to pay Beethoven an annual salary of one thousand five hundred ducats, with Prince Lobkowitz con-

Countess Anna Marie Erdödy, née Nitzky. Miniature on ivory.

tributing seven hundred, and Prince Kinsky eighteen hundred florins—all of them "for life."

Beethoven's immediate reaction to this arrangement was to make plans for several journeys: first to Leipzig; then with the tenor Röckel—his first Florestan—to the major German cities; as well as to England and Spain. However, though he never abandoned the idea of undertaking a "cultural journey" he never in fact went through with any of his plans. He then wrote to Gleichenstein, who had gone to visit his family in the Black Forest: "Now you can help me to find a wife!" It is more than likely that he already had quite definite ideas about this subject when he wrote these words. His physician, Dr. Schmidt, had died the previous year and was replaced by a Dr. Malfatti, who had two attractive nieces, Anna—who was engaged to Zmeskall—and Therese. Even before the signing of the contract he had written that quiet yet melodious Cello Sonata, op. 69, for Gleichenstein, to whom he dedicated it "inter lacrimas et luctum," as was also the case with the two piano trios dedicated to the lady of the house, Countess Erdödy. These are all cheerful, good-tempered works, containing no more than a trace of the longing present in the four settings to Goethe's poem "Nur wer die Sehnsucht kennt" that he had composed shortly before this. One last time we find accounts in several letters of his active playing: "I enjoy playing so much"—with Zmeskall for instance, whom he refers to as "that dear old music-making count." He is also known to have played with Schuppanzigh, the skilled cellist, Kraft, and with Countess Erdödy—until such time as she incurred his displeasure when he found out that she used to give his servant a tip to prevent him from running away. He was again beset by anxieties. Hence we read of the high level of prices as a result of the lost war, and Beethoven finding himself forced to ask Simrock for a loan "because of our current situation."

NOTHING BUT WOUNDS

At this moment political events made themselves more force-fully felt than ever. The occupation of Vienna in 1805—at the time of the *Fidelio* première—was followed by the Peace of Schönbrunn, which in turn sparked off the rivalry between the German princes to win Napoleon's favor, and caused Franz II to abdicate the imperial throne. Beethoven carefully referred to the campaign against the Prussians in a letter to Härtel as "the events in your country," and the news of Napoleon's victory at Jena is reputed to have led him to exclaim: "What a pity that I do not understand the art of war as well as I do the art of composition, for I would certainly beat him!" At the beginning of April, shortly after it became known that Beethoven had de-clined the offer to go to Cassel, Napoleon opened his new cam-paign, and it became impossible to protect Vienna from attack. The bombardment of the town by the French in May drove Beethoven to take refuge in the cellar of his brother's house, where he attempted to protect his over-sensitive ears with cush-ions. At the end of July, his publisher in Leipzig received a letter containing the following remarks: "You are indeed mistaken if you think I have been well, for we have been suffering extreme misery in recent times. Let me tell you that since May 4 I have produced precious little coherent work—in fact nothing more than the odd fragment here and there. The whole course of events has affected me personally in both a physical and a mental way; I still cannot even enjoy to the full the pleasures of country life that are so indispensable to me. The existence I had built up for myself only a short time ago rests on shaky ground ... Heaven knows what is going to happen ... The levies are beginning this very day. What a destructive, confused life I see around me! Nothing but drums, cannons and human misery of all kinds." He resumed his activities gradually with a number of small tasks. The piano introduction to the *Choral Fantasy* that he had improvised at the concert in December now took final form. A partiality for stricter rhythms was confirmed in a march commissioned by the new Master of the Teutonic Order, though

Therese von Brunswick. Oil Portrait by Johann Baptist Lampi the Elder, 1806.

it was subsequently dedicated to the "Bohemian militia," and was known generally as the *Yorck* March.

He was probably also involved with the commission that was handed over the following year to Archduke Rudolf as "the desired horse music with the quickest gallop." To the proposal to try out its effect on the horses he commented: "By all means! I want to see if the riders can do agile somersaults or not. I have to laugh at the thought that Your Majesty will be reminded of me even then . . ." But it was only on returning to Baden after a stay in the country that he was able to get back into a suitable work routine again. Having achieved this, he composed simultaneously the *Lebewohl* Sonata, the last Piano Concerto, and the Harp Quartet in E flat major op. 74. Also dating from the same year are the six Variations in D major op. 76 on the Theme of a Turkish March, for his "loyal friend" Oliva; the great Fantasy for Piano op. 77 for Franz von Brunswick; the Sonata in D sharp major for Therese von Brunsvik; various incidental pieces; and finally the "classical" overture for *Egmont* of 1809/10. Rather regretfully we then hear of various plans which seem to be temporarily dictated by patriotism; for instance the projected battle portrait, and the military anthem "Österreich über alles" to a text by Collin. Events soon took their full course, and he quickly found his old equilibrium again.

According to one Baron de Trémont, a Frenchman who was received by Beethoven solely on the strength of a letter of recommendation from Anton Reicha, it would have taken a Dickens or a Balzac to give an accurate description of Beethoven's person and clothing. The first account of their meeting published after his death may be unreliable in some respects, but it does nevertheless contain comments which correspond with the descriptions given by others: that he was "a very ugly and bad-tempered man," "that his improvisations were probably the most powerful musical impressions" that he (Trémont) had ever experienced. He then recounts how they discussed philosophy, religion, politics, and particularly his idol Shakespeare: ". . . Beethoven was no wit . . . being too quiet by nature . . . His thoughts came in fits and starts. He was always broad-minded and generous, though not infrequently mistaken . . . very well read . . . he has studied the classics . . . His playing contained errors . . . I asked him if he would not like to go to get to know France . . ." Beethoven's reply to the invitation was that he had "always wanted to do so very much indeed . . . before it landed itself with an emperor." Trémont goes on to state that at the Austrian court Beethoven was considered to be an outspoken republican, and that the court proper did not patronize him at all. ". . . He had at one time absolutely worshipped Napoleon . . . yet he was extremely worried by Napoleon's love of grandeur." Trémont also refers to Beethoven's intimate life, mentioning among others the names of Giulietta Guicciardi and Countess Erdödy, and finishing with the mysterious sentence: ". . . I know the third object of his passion, but I may not name it." Much of what Trémont wrote was corroborated almost to the word by Reichardt, who saw Beethoven frequently both at concerts and at musical sessions in private houses: "lucky is the artist who can be certain of such an audience . . ."

In the meantime, yet another change of management had taken place in the court theater. That September, while Napoleon was in Vienna, at the request of the new director Beethoven conducted a performance of his *Eroica* Symphony at a large charity concert. But the "hero" for whom the work had originally been intended left the city the very day before the concert.

Perhaps as a result of this concert Beethoven was then given the commission to compose some incidental music for Goethe's *Egmont.* His preparations for this task lasted until June 1810, accompanied by various personal vicissitudes. Songs such as

Clärchen's "Freudvoll und leidvoll" convey much of his own personal heartache. In March 1809 Albrechtsberger died, followed in April by the young wife of his friend Breuning, and in May by Haydn, the latter shortly after the bombardment of the city, so that he was already buried before the news of his death could be made known. In Gleichenstein's absence his duties as Beethoven's factotum were taken over first of all by Zmeskall, and then by Franz Oliva, who was probably the son of a horn-player in the Esterházy orchestra. An educated young man, experienced in matters of business and finance, he was to make himself useful in dealing with Beethoven's correspondence for a good many years to come. He conducted negotiations with publishers and made the necessary arrangements for concerts and other performances, for which he was rewarded—like Gleichenstein and Zmeskall—with a dedication. Due to some argument Beethoven did not return to Countess Erdödy's house after his short stay in the country, but took new rooms, first of all in the Walfischgasse and subsequently in the "Klepperstall." The rapid change of temperature led to fresh outbreaks of his old complaint—inflammation of the bowel—in December and again in January 1810. The political situation caused a deterioration of conditions in general. The blowing up of the city ramparts aggravated his ear troubles, which drove him to remonstrate: "Confound the war! If I had not read somewhere that a man should not voluntarily quit this life so long as he can still perform a good deed, I should have left this world long ago—and what is more, by my own hand" (May 1810 in a letter to Wegeler). Somewhat unexpectedly he then received two hundred pounds sterling in payment for the score he had delivered to Clementi three years previously. Gleichenstein, who had in the meantime returned to Vienna, was immediately delegated to buy him a new supply of underwear, neckcloths, and so on. His tailor received three hundred florins in payment of an outstanding bill. He then returned to his old apartment in Baron Pasqualati's house. From the fact that he appears at the time to have been in frequent need of Zmeskall's advice it can be deduced that he was in love once again. That it was more serious this time than ever before can be seen easily from a letter he wrote to Wegeler in which he asked the latter to get hold of his baptismal certificate because the "family book" had been mislaid. Sundry letters to Gleichenstein around this time give more grounds for guesswork than actual facts: "My greetings to all who are dear to you and to me. How gladly would I add, and to whom we are dear?? This question mark applies at any rate to me . . . Be happy . . . I am not happy . . ." And again he goes on: "Since I haven't got enough time this morning, I am coming to the 'Wild Man' in the Prater at midday, though I suspect I shall not find wild men but graceful beauties there . . . If I could meet you this morning . . . anywhere you care to mention . . . Herewith the sonata that I have promised to Therese . . . Give my regards to all of them, I feel so at home with them . . . It is as if the wounds with which my soul has been lacerated by various malicious people could be healed again through her." And finally, in a letter to the woman in question, Therese Malfatti: "Beloved Therese, you receive with this letter that which I promised to send you. No doubt I should be placing my hopes too high or overestimating my worth if I were to say, in the words of the old adage, that people are united not only when actually together; even the distant one or the departed one is present with us. Who would apply such a saying to our volatile Therese who treats life so lightheartedly? . . . I am leading a very quiet and lonely life here. Although now and then lights would like to wake me, since you all left Vienna a void has grown within me that cannot be filled . . . Commend me to the goodwill of your father and mother, though as yet I can rightly make no claim to it . . . Forget my mad behavior . . . Rest assured that no one can wish

Therese von Malfatti.

you a happier and gayer life than I, and that I desire it even if
you take no interest whatever . . ."

In much the same vein are the lines he wrote to Gleichenstein: ". . . embrace them all, every heart . . . why can mine not
be among them? . . . the letter is written in such a way that the
whole world can read it . . ." A note of uncertainty sets in: "You
live on a quiet, peaceful lake, or already in a safe harbor . . . the

need for a friend that is experienced by the man in the middle of a storm is a feeling you do not know . . . What will they think of me on another planet, how will they judge me without seeing me . . . my pride is so humiliated . . . if you could only be more frank—you are definitely withholding something from me—you want to protect me, and yet you give me the pain of this uncertainty . . . I cannot commit to paper any more of these thoughts that are going through my head . . ." The decision seems to have come quickly: "Your news has again plunged me from the most sublime ecstasy down into the deepest depths. And why did you add that remark that you would let me know when there would be music again? Am I then nothing more than a musicmaker for yourself and the others? . . . No, friendship and the emotions related with it bring nothing but wounds for me. Well, so be it. For you, poor Beethoven, no happiness can come from outside. You must create your world within yourself. Only in the world of ideas will you find friends—I beg you to set my mind at rest by telling me whether I personally was to blame yesterday . . ." Beethoven's relationship with Therese is recorded in various documents, such as the copy of "Mignon's Song" begun by Therese herself, which Beethoven completed and furnished with the comment: "N. B.: the author has dared to bring to light Fräulein Therese's improvements to this song." Further information is provided by the papers and letters once in her possession, including among others "Clärchen's Song," and it is fairly certain that the title of the well-known piece for piano *Für Elise* should in fact read *Für Therese*.

Therese, who was more than twenty years younger than Beethoven, was married only a few years after this to Baron von Drosdick, one of the Privy Councilors. She was to survive Beethoven by over twenty years. Though her name is mentioned subsequently on one occasion only, it is believed that the String Quartet op. 95, which was composed that summer, is a reflection

Bettina von Arnim. Etching by Ludwig Emil Grimm.

of the feelings that overwhelmed him after the collapse of his hopes. A short time later Breuning informed Wegeler that he believed that Beethoven's "hoped-for marriage" had fallen through.

But that same May—or possibly at the very beginning of June—at a moment when he was "totally oppressed by ill-humor," he happened to meet another woman, who not without justification qualifies as the most renowned of all the women in Beethoven's life—Bettina Brentano. Though already married to Achim von Arnim, and considerably younger than the composer, she had a gifted lyrical and musical imagination which made her an ideal conversationalist for him. Although only "groping in her emotions" and "describing pictorially," she nevertheless interpreted without inhibition anything and everything that happened to her. Her verbal descriptions of these impressions hence seem somewhat dubious. As sister of "one of the noblest of men," Franz Brentano, she took rooms in a house well-known to Beethoven, and whenever she wanted to see him it was enough for her name to be mentioned to him, and she was received with open arms. Despite the fact that she is suspected of having embellished and stylized two (if not more) of the three letters she is thought to have received from Beethoven (along the lines of her fictional *Goethe's Correspondence with a Child*), and despite the fact that she was partly responsible for the "romanticization" of Beethoven's image, he himself was clearly impressed to an extraordinarily strong degree by her personality. Goethe's own words to Beethoven in a letter dated June 25, 1811 also confirm that she admired him as no one else had done: "Sweet Bettina Brentano really deserves the interest you have shown her. She is quite ecstatically taken with you, and counts the hours she spent with you as some of the happiest of her whole life." Equally authentic is the letter she wrote to Anton Bihler, a pupil of her brother-in-law, Friedrich von Savigny. Leaving aside the description of his apartment, there are still plenty of relevant observations: "He is small in stature . . . tanned, covered with pock-marks —in a word, repulsive. But he has a heavenly forehead." Only with difficulty did she persuade him to play for her: "Suddenly he becomes oblivious of everything about him. When he has been composing he is quite deaf, and his eyes stare confusedly at the outside world . . . so that he lives in deepest isolation . . . He starts by drawing up a comprehensive plan, and arranges his music in along certain lines from which he then works. . . . But why do I write this? Because I . . . believe that both you and I have feeling and admiration for such a disposition . . . and because I know how unjustly people speak of him, simply because they are too narrow-minded to be able to understand him . . ." An indisputable piece of evidence for Beethoven's own impressions of the hours he spent with Bettina is to be found in his letter to her of February 10, 1811: "I carried your first letter about with me the whole summer, and it often made me feel supremely happy . . . But what should I tell you about myself? 'Pity my fate,' I cry with Johanna [a quotation from Schiller's *Jungfrau von Orleans*] . . . As for my affection, the sister has such a large share of it that not much will be left for her brother . . . All good wishes, dear Bettina. I kiss you on your forehead and imprint on it, as with a seal, all my thoughts for you.—Write soon, soon, and very often to your dear friend Beethoven." Bettina can be credited with having brought about the meeting between Beethoven and Goethe, though to her dismay some annoyance on Goethe's part resulted in her personally not being present. No such shadow ever overcast her relationship with the "friendless" Beethoven, probably all the more so since their friendship never exceeded the bounds of an "elective affinity" or Platonic attachment.

In May Beethoven was still in Vienna. Though he himself had probably wanted to go to the country much sooner, his "master," Archduke Rudolf, who was in residence at Schönbrunn, wanted to have Beethoven near him. In addition, as he wrote to Zmeskall: "new demands from friends every day, new acquaintances, new relationships . . . sometimes I could almost go mad with this unearned fame of mine. Fortune is seeking me out, and precisely for this reason I almost fear that another misfortune will befall me . . . I hope that when we see each other again you will find that my art has improved with time." But in mid-July, just when the first batch of Scottish songs was ready for the printer, he was still in Vienna. Finally, in August, having completed extensive corrections to the manuscript, and with an additional payment of two thousand florins from Kinsky in his pocket, he was eventually able to set off for his beloved Baden. Even there he was chiefly preoccupied with plans for publications—including the proposed authorized general edition of his works to be published by Breitkopf & Härtel. He then briefly considered the idea of renting rooms with a farmer there for the winter, on account of his "wretched ears," and to leave behind him once and for all the troublesome noise and bustle of city life. But he soon discovered for himself that "without the company of some dear human being, it would be quite impossible to live in the country." It was here that he gathered ideas for his Piano Trio in B flat major op. 97, a "pastorale per camera"—his last and finest work in the genre and probably one of the greatest works in existence.

By the end of March 1811 he had completed op. 97, and this was followed by a "creative pause." In August he was still caught up in correspondence with publishers. The settings of the English songs he was doing at this time for George Thomson cannot really be considered a creative production worthy of him. Though Beethoven was probably following the conditions of the original contract of November 1806, the whole affair was nevertheless curious enough. Thomson had sent him the first forty-three Welsh and Irish songs, minus texts, in 1809, for which ritornellos and instrumental settings were required. The relevant texts were to be arranged by the publisher without collaboration with the composer. In some instances there was not even an indication of the mood of the particular song. Similar contracts for Thomson had previously been undertaken by Kozeluch and Pleyel, and later by Haydn and Carl Maria von Weber. Beethoven completed in all more than one hundred and twenty-five such settings. Since the subject as a whole stimulated him to search out non-English material, his song settings also include, for example, Tyrolean songs. Having left Thomson in no doubt that the contract was a task that "gave an artist no particular joy," he countered the publisher's repeated

Bad Teplitz, around 1806.

requests for "a lighter touch" with demands for a "heavier fee."

Rheumatic troubles that year drove him to look for a more invigorating spa. The desire to meet Goethe at long last made him settle on Teplitz. Franz Oliva had already gone off to Leipzig in April, where he was conducting negotiations on Beethoven's behalf with Breitkopf & Härtel. From there he proceeded to Weimar to deliver a letter from Beethoven to Goethe which contained the following introduction: ". . . the opportunity afforded me by a friend of mine and great admirer of yours (as I am also), who is leaving Vienna very soon, allows me only a moment in which to thank you for the long time that I have known you (for I have known you since my childhood)—That is so little for so much—Bettina Brentano has assured me that you would receive me kindly, indeed as a friend . . . You will shortly receive my music for *Egmont* . . . and I should very much like to have your opinion on it—even your disapproval would be useful to me, and I would welcome it as much as the highest praise . . ." As he did not want to travel alone on account of his bad hearing, Beethoven had apparently hoped that Franz von Brunswick would accompany him on the journey to Teplitz, but the latter found himself prevented from leaving Vienna, as a result of which their departure had to be delayed until August. Meanwhile Oliva seems to have been waiting for him in Teplitz, and on Beethoven's arrival was able to introduce him to the circle of stimulating people also on holiday at the spa. They included, among others, the young writer Varnhagen von Ense and his witty companion Rahel Levin; the poet Tiedge, whose poem "An die Hoffnung" ("Ode to Hope") was a particular favorite of Beethoven; and Countess von der Recke, the authoress and friend of Tiege. Rahel seems to have fascinated Beethoven greatly, and she had no difficulty in persuading him to play for the company, and possibly even to accompany the Berlin soprano, Amalie Sebald, who was there with the Countess. It was probably more out of the wish to remain in contact with Rahel that Beethoven allowed himself to be talked into translating and adapting a French melodrama. Perhaps he showed her the score of the oratorio which was then at the printers, and it is also possible that he brought with him Kotzebue's *The Ruins of Athens* and *King Stephen* for which he had to compose the incidental music in time for the opening of the newly built Pester Theater. Since the day foreseen for this occasion was October 4, the name day of the Kaiser, he could not stay on indefinitely at Teplitz. On the return journey he is reputed to have run into Prince Lichnowsky in Grätz—though it is far more likely that he in fact stayed with Count Oppersdorf instead, in order to hear the performance of his C major Mass in nearby Troppau, where he is said to have amazed the audience by extemporizing on the organ afterwards.

Work on the two Kotzebue plays demanded all his creative energies until well into September—which was not all that long a time for the composition of two overtures and seventeen individual numbers. They contain a good deal more than one might assume, in view of the fact that they were never performed. It is also known that he even asked Kotzbue to write an opera libretto for him: "Let it be romantic, serious, sentimental, or a mixture of heroic and comic—in fact best of all, some great historical theme . . . in particular from the Dark Ages, for instance from the time of Attila the Hun . . ." The Pester Theater festivities however had to be postponed until the following February, and Beethoven thus found the time to indulge in a bit of social life again. There are reports of him dining with Zmeskall and von Brunswick, best of all at his favorite "Swan Inn," that is, whenever he was not invited to dinner by the Breunings. Notes from the time, peppered with strong language, indicate the duality, the conflict between appearance and reality within his personality. "Many people enjoy watching a heroic play without having anything in common with it whatever," he wrote to Therese von Brunswick. One minute he was storming at Zmeskall that he was "a confounded, petty music-making count" followed by sundry other similar abusive terms, while the next moment he had effected a complete change of mood—and mind—declaring himself to be "devishly well disposed towards him" which in the next breath had even progressed as far as "confoundedly devoted." He still held a predominantly pessimistic view towards his own situation in life, as an indication of which the word "unfortunately" appears constantly in his letters and writings. The sixteen hundred florins allowed him by his contract had dwindled as a result of the so-called "fiscal patent" to such an extent that Beethoven referred to himself at this time as "a poor Austrian musician," and was forced to make even more efforts to sell his works. Luck favored him for the moment, and Breitkopf & Härtel published all his works from op. 69 to op. 86. In 1810 to 1811 alone almost two dozen impressions of his works

Prince Ferdinand Kinsky. Lithograph by Josef Kriehuber.

appeared, including the *Egmont* and *Leonora* Overtures. Shortly
before the completion of the Seventh Symphony in May 1812
he informed Härtel that he had already begun work on several
other symphonies. At this time he was also making preparations for a second visit to Teplitz, a visit which was to be far
more memorable than the first. By July 2 he had already
reached Prague, where he was received by Prince Kinsky and
discussed the latter's part of the contract allowance. Franz Oliva
had already written about this problem to Varnhagen, and had
succeeded in getting Kinsky to agree to the more advantageous
method of the archducal mode of payment, but neglected to
obtain Kinsky's written statement to that effect. Three days
later Beethoven arrived at Teplitz to find the entire Napoleonic
court, including Empress Josephine and numerous officials, in

residence there. Almost simultaneously the French armies started on the long march to Russia.

From the visitors' book we know that the same year Lichnowsky, Goethe, the Brentanos, Achim von Armin, Varnhagen, Tiedge, von Savigny, and Frau Sebald and her daughter were also in Teplitz—though not all at the same time, as they tended to move from spa to spa according to the nature of the specific cure prescribed for them. And Beethoven did likewise: at the end of July he left Teplitz for Karlsbad, and on August 8 moved on again to Franzensbad near Eger, returning a month later to Teplitz. There he chose to ignore the "aristocratic vermin," if his own words are to be believed, and even complained that there were "not so many interesting people present as last year." Both Tiedge and Countess von der Recke had already departed by the

Goethe, 1819. Portrait by Georg Dawe.

time he arrived. But then at long last came the meeting with Goethe. Bettina Brentano had married Achim von Arnim and had become in Goethe's eyes "a tiresome horsefly" after she had insulted his wife Christiane. Her remarks, which are in any case contradictory—especially about the conversations between writer and composer—are extremely untrustworthy. We know for certain that Goethe did not arrive until mid-July, that Beethoven visited him for the first time on July 19 and that during that conversation they agreed to go for a walk to Bilin the following day. We know, too, that they spent at least the evenings of July 21 and July 23 together in Beethoven's apartment, and there he played many of his works on the piano to Goethe's clearly stated delight. It was Goethe's opinion that "the dignity of art . . . appears perhaps most supremely of all in music because it does not have to deal with any subject matter." In a letter to Karl Zelter he made the following statements on Beethoven: "His talent astonishes me. Unfortunately, though, he is an utterly untamed personality. While he is not wholly unjustified in holding the world to be detestable, he does not make it any the more enjoyable either for himself or for other people by his attitude. On the other hand, he is very much to be excused and pitied as his hearing is forsaking him, which perhaps has a more immediately negative effect on his social rather than his musical life. He is in any case of a laconic nature, and will undoubtedly become doubly so because of this deficiency." Beethoven's own reflections on the encounter are far scantier, as can be seen from a letter to the Archduke in which he stated quite simply: "I spent a lot of time together with Goethe." And again to his Leipzig publisher: "Goethe is too fond of the atmosphere of the courts, more so than is becoming in a poet." But some ten years later we find the comment made by one of his friends to the effect that "he is a great admirer of Goethe, and likes to think of the time he spent with the famous poet in Karlsbad."

A series of eight cheerful letters to Amalie Sebald testifies to a harmless flirtation he indulged in that autumn for a short time, possibly as a reaction to an experience encountered on his homeward journey which in turn is said to be connected with the most moving document of his passion—the letter addressed "to the immortal beloved." Granted, there is much doubt about this document on account of its incomplete and possibly even misleading date. The additional fact that it was found, together with seven bank shares and the portrait of Therese Brunswick, in a secret drawer of his wardrobe, in no way clarifies whether it was either never sent, whether it was returned, or whether for some reason or other it could not be delivered. It is hardly surprising that every single woman Beethoven ever knew has at some point been considered as the probable recipient of this letter, although not much would actually be gained by establishing the identity of the woman in question. Even though we have to be satisfied with an extremely sketchy picture of her personality, it would be absolutely impossible to speculate about any possible effects the affair might have had on Beethoven's life and work. In the thirteen letters to Josephine Deym, the sister of Franz and Therese Brunswick, there is indeed a frequent occurrence of phrases such as: "Dear J! How much I hope that you might care to give me the happiness of your love. I am not drawn to you solely by the attraction I feel towards the opposite sex; no, it is your whole self, with all your idiosyncrasies, that has won my esteem, my feelings and all my perceptive faculties." Although these letters date from the years when Josephine was already the widowed mother of four children, remarks by both sisters in letters and diaries indicate that the relationship between Josephine and Beethoven must have been more than a mere friendship. The youngest Brunswick sister, Charlotte, found it "un peu dangereux" that Beethoven came to visit her sister every day, especially as he had been treated with such enthusiastic deference ever since he was first introduced to the mother and two elder sisters in 1799. Josephine had been married off somewhat hastily (after knowing the man for only four weeks) to a certain Count Deym, who was almost thirty years her senior. The marriage was not a happy one. Deym died in 1804, when it is known that Therese—who according to another member of the household was herself once engaged to Beethoven—insisted that Josephine should "have the strength to say no." She eventually married again, probably for the sake of her children, on February 14, 1810, her second husband being a Baron von Stackelberg who was employed in the service of the Russians. The two had already decided to separate shortly before Beethoven's arrival in Prague in July 1812, so it is just possible that Beethoven's excuse to Varnhagen of "an unforeseen circumstance . . . that prevents me from spending my last evening in Prague with you" might have been connected with a meeting with Josephine.

The hypothesis that Josephine must be the recipient of the letter in question rests on the slenderest and most circumstantial evidence. Still, the setting to Teidge's poem "An die Hoffnung" was composed in her honor, and it is also known that when the copy he made for her found its way by mistake into the hands of Prince Lichnowsky in 1805, Beethoven had to calm her down. In Teplitz, at the time when the letter in question was written, some of the wording would have had particular relevance. "Why this profound sorrow when necessity speaks . . . Can you alter the fact that you are not wholly mine, that I am not wholly yours? . . . Love demands all, and rightly so, and thus it is for me with you and for you with me . . . If we were completely united, you would feel this painful necessity as much as I do . . . The gods must decide our fate . . . / You are suffering, my most precious one . . . / my thoughts rush to you, my immortal beloved . . . I can live only with you or not at all . . . Be calm, for only by calmly considering our lives can we achieve our aim

Countess Josephine Deym, née von Brunswick. Anonymous Miniature.

to live together . . . ever yours—ever mine—ever ours, L."
When, after Beethoven's death, the letter was shown to Therese,
she had no doubt whatever that it was intended for her sister.
She is reputed to have said: "What would she not have turned
our hero into—Josephine's friend in house and heart! They were
born for each other, and were they both still alive, they would
have been united." A daughter, Minona, to whom Josephine

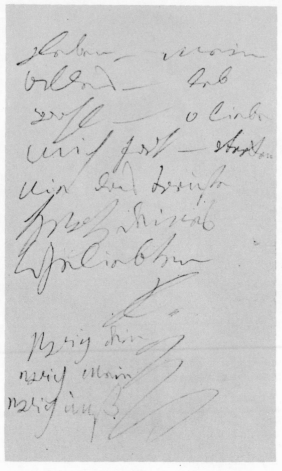

Last page of the letter to the "immortal beloved."

gave birth on April 8 in the following year, is supposed to have
looked very different from her other children, and to have been
cared for with especially loving attention by Therese in the home
she opened in Hungary for eighty homeless children. Further-
more, a certain Fräulein von Stackelberg, though it is not certain
whether this was Minona or not, is known to have carried out

arrangements of contemporary piano works. Josephine died in 1821. Beethoven's grief was very great, as was observed by Therese. In his own journal we then find the following confession: "Submission, absolute submission to your fate! . . . Oh hard struggle! . . . I may not live for myself, but only for others. For me there can be no happiness anymore except in myself, in my art . . ." And again in May 1813: "Oh terrible circumstances that do not suppress my longing for family life . . . Oh God! . . . please do not let it go on like this much longer!"

He had barely arrived back in Vienna—apparently cured of the illness that had ultimately hindered him from seeing much of Amalie Sebald—when he received the news that caused him to ask Gleichenstein to find out the quickest and cheapest way of getting to Linz. As early as October 5 it was made known that Beethoven—"the Orpheus and greatest musician of our time"—had arrived in town. His brother Johann, the chemist, had taken as his housekeeper the sister-in-law of a doctor who was living in the same house. She already had a daughter from a previous liaison. The question is whether Beethoven's visit was in response to an invitation to the wedding or whether he in fact came to prevent it taking place at all. Only years later do we read in one of his conversation books: "My brother's marriage proved both his immorality and his lack of judgment . . ." At all events, he avoided creating any kind of sensation while in Linz, played in the house of a musically inclined count, composed three funeral cantatas for All Souls' Day for the cathedral orchestra, and completed the first draft of the Eighth Symphony.

The wedding finally took place when Beethoven had been in Linz for five weeks, and just two days later he returned to Vienna in order to be present at the opening of the season. That December the Violin Sonata op. 96 was played for the first time by Pierre Rode, for whom it had been written, and the Archduke. It was to surpass all others in popularity. From this same

Bust of Beethoven by Franz Klein, 1812.

period dates the famous bust of him by Franz Klein. It was based on a life mask, during the making of which Beethoven was convinced he was going to suffocate. The last letter of this tempestuous year contained the tragic news that the thirty-one-year-old Prince Kinsky had suddenly died. Beethoven was most deeply affected by the mourning for the prince.

The next two and a half years saw the dénouement of Napoleon's attempts to dominate Europe being played out from Moscow to Waterloo. Beethoven's symphony in commemoration of the Battle of Waterloo was rightly never included in the ranks of his "immortal" creations. During this whole period he was almost always ill. Life seemed to be one long series of complaints: about the outstanding payments due on contracts, about an academy concert that never came off, and so on. Because of the war, the only entertainments permitted were the charity concerts in which he occasionally took part, also a tragedy, *Tarpeja,* which was put on for the benefit of Mozart's brother-in-law, Joseph Lange. It was about this time, too, that he struck up a friendship with Johann Mälzel, the ingenious technician who invented among other things a mechanical trumpet and an automatic harmonium which he called a "panharmonicon." Mälzel was continually on the search for the "most effective symphonic melody," so the two men started to make plans together which were to culminate in a projected cultural visit to England. At the end of May Beethoven traveled repeatedly between Baden and the piano factory where Mälzel was conducting his experiments. It was the latter's idea to represent Wellington's victory at Vittoria by the drum marches and bugle-calls of the enemy troops, including also "Rule Britannia" and "God Save the King." By November Beethoven had all the scores ready, and the first two performances held that December brought in a clear profit of four thousand florins in aid of Austrian soldiers wounded at Hanau. The two repeat performances in January and February brought in similarly good takings. The general atmosphere of excitement, increased still more by the news of Napoleon's defeat at Leipzig and the recently effected retreat over the Rhine, contributed greatly to the triumphal jubilation accorded to the symphony. The applause was by all accounts quite fantastic—even if the experts of the musical world were absolutely amazed at this "deviation of his muse."

Some misunderstanding had led to a sudden rift with Mälzel which came to a head when the latter succeeded behind Beethoven's back in getting hold of the entire score of the *Battle Symphony* (as *Wellington's Victory* was otherwise known) and had it published in Munich. With the revenue he obtained from this enterprise Mälzel was able to finance his planned journey to London. Despite countless difficulties Beethoven immediately managed to send off a copy dedicated to the English Prince Regent, which was never even acknowledged, let alone remunerated—a fact that he never got over all his life. In Vienna, however, this work brought him the most extraordinary popularity. There was a sudden rush for everything he had ever composed, and his works were performed countless times in concerts organized by various societies and organizations, as also in academy and charity concerts. The growing interest in Beethoven's music worked out particularly well for *Fidelio* which was then requested by the management of the Hoftheater. Beethoven agreed on the condition that he be allowed to revise it thoroughly. At the end of June he is reputed to have stated that "hardly a single piece of the music is the same, and more than half the opera has been entirely rewritten." Unexpectedly, the new burst of creativity also brought about an increase in his self-confidence: "If they want me, they can have me, and then I shall still have the freedom to say yes or no. Freedom! What more can one have than freedom?" After Napoleon's defeat he was occupied chiefly with a variety of smaller compositions, in-

Beethoven in 1814. Engraving by Blasius Höfel after Louis Letronne.

cluding one for a town councilor, one in honor of Dr. Malfatti, and finally some *Elegiac Songs* for his landlord, Baron Pasqualati. The second half of the year was dominated by the festivities in connection with the Congress of Vienna. First of all he turned his attention to a cantata in honor of the allied princes, *Ihr weisen Gründer glücklicher Staaten,* which he followed up with another cantata *Der glorreiche Augenblick: Europa steht,* the printed score of which fills two hundred sides, as well as various canons and songs. April saw the first performances of these new works, including that by Schuppanzigh of the new Piano Trio op. 97. Ingaz Moscheles, who subsequently became a famous piano composer, complained about the "lack of purity and precision" of Beethoven's keyboard technique. Though he did admit that it still contained "many traces of great playing," the end result was that Beethoven played in public very rarely after this time. Towards the end of May 1814 the revised version of *Fidelio* went into rehearsal at the Kärnthnerthor Theater, still without the new overture which, according to his physician, Dr. Bertolini, Beethoven composed on the back of a menu at an inn, but failed to finish in time. On the day of the first performance Beethoven was acclaimed enthusiastically and called for by the audience right from the first act on. By October of that year the opera had been staged sixteen times, and in November it was produced in Prague under the direction of Carl Maria von Weber. In addition to various incidental pieces he also composed a piano sonata (op. 90) for Prince Lichnowsky's brother, Count Moritz. Then, with the opening of the Congress there began the glittering series of concerts and social events staged in honor of the assembled princes. These included several performances in the apartments of the Archduke, where Beethoven's cantata and the two new symphonies were greeted with enthusiasm by a festive audience.

The receptions, soirées and balls continued nonstop well into the new year. At the end of January the birthday of the German-born Russian empress was celebrated with great splendor in the castle. On this occasion Beethoven himself accompanied the Fidelio quartet, and at a private audience handed to the Czarina the polonaise he had composed in her honor, as well as other works arranged especially for her. For his negotiations with her court officials Zmeskall received the following directions: "Should Her Majesty wish to hear me play, I would be only too honored, but I must first of all ask Her to bear with me, since for quite some time now I have devoted myself exclusively to composition . . ." In March his oratorio was performed again. But on June 15, at the news of Napoleon's defeat at Waterloo and subsequent exile, the illustrious company in Vienna dispersed.

When Beethoven discovered that *Wellington's Victory* had been performed by Sir George Smart in London, he took the opportunity of making an offer to Smart—with the banker Johann von Häring helping him over the English—in the hopes that at least some of the works composed in the previous four years might be published in London. Häring remarks that Beethoven spoke continually of going to England, but he feared that his deafness would not permit it. An overture for the Emperor's name day was not finished in time, and was only heard for the first time in December, together with the cantata *Meeresstille und glückliche Fahrt,* which was dedicated to Goethe. In connection with this latter work Beethoven was praised for his "philanthropic support" in donating it free of charge.

With the breakup of the Congress Vienna's days of glory came to an end and it drifted into the state of "torpid graveyard tranquility" that so often results from a financial depression: a situation that was to last far beyond Beethoven's own lifetime. In March he broke off all business relations with Breitkopf & Härtel after a dispute over ways of raising money, and was then forced to come to an agreement with a publisher in Vienna. Al-

121

most concurrently with the offer to Sir George Smart he also succeeded in drawing up terms with the publishing house of Sigmund Anton Steiner, who from this time on was his favorite publisher. In April Steiner agreed to take thirteen works including the *Fidelio* score and the three new overtures. Beethoven declared that he was "completely satisfied" with the arrangement, and reserved only the English rights for himself. Soon after this Tobias Haslinger entered Steiner's business as a director and

Portrait by Willibrord Mähler, 1815.

music dealer. He became extremely dedicated to Beethoven, and knew better than anyone how to handle him. His office in the Paternostergasse rapidly became the meeting place for members of the musical world of Vienna, and many a conversation begun there was subsequently continued in the neighboring inns and cafés.

Even after the close of the Congress, Vienna remained the most sought-after destination for visitors from all over the world. It goes without saying that no traveler interested in music wanted to leave the city without having seen Beethoven. Haslinger's office at times contained as many as fifty people or more, all waiting for the great man himself to appear. Even when he was out in the country, Tobias brought many an important guest out to see him. In 1815 he was again in Baden, where he composed the two cello sonatas of op. 102 and possibly also the Variations for Piano Trio on Wenzel Müller's song "Ich bin der Schneider Kakadu." From Baden he was able to visit Countess Erdödy in nearby Jedlersee on the other side of the Danube, but a year later the Countess was then forced for unknown reasons to leave Austria. Prince Lichnowsky having died the previous year, Beethoven had to leave his old home on the Mölker Bastei (one of the ramparts of Vienna). From then on the management of his household affairs was taken over by Frau Nanette Streicher. She even found him a new apartment, apparently very close to the Archduke's residence, to which Beethoven is supposed to have commented to his patron: "I took the apartment, thinking Your Imperial Highness would refund me a small part of it, otherwise I would not have taken it." Although new ideas continued to flow and he made a great many notes and sketches, the years 1815 and 1816 in the end produced nothing but the song cycle "An die ferne Geliebte," op. 98, the Piano Sonata op. 101, and various smaller pieces such as canons and the Scottish songs. For a while he again nurtured the thought of writing another opera, and considered in turn *Bacchus, Romulus,* and *Pennsylvania* as possible themes. His notes from the time contain a number of remarks relating to the project such as: "Dissonances perhaps not resolved throughout the opera; B minor key; to devise the best opening movement based on harmony." And finally: "Every day someone to dinner, like Musici, and we discuss this and that." He was probably not unpleased to see the long announced young Englishman, Charles Neate, from the London Philharmonic Society, with whom he strolled through the summer woods. From these days dates his confession: "Almighty God, I am so happy in the woods, every tree speaks through You . . ."

Only in mid-October did he return to the city, where he had to give precedence to publishing matters. Just a month later he stood shattered with grief at the bier of his brother Karl, who had died after a short illness of tuberculosis at the relatively young age of thirty-eight. On Beethoven's instructions his physician, Dr. Bertolini, had to establish "whether the end had been precipitated by poison or not." The suspicion proved groundless, but it is indicative of Beethoven's feeling of distrust towards his sister-in-law, the "queen of the night" as he called her—and with reason. Karl's will had long since made provision that in the case of his death, Ludwig should act as guardian to his only son, also called Karl. However, at the last moment he had added the codicil that on no account did he want his son to be removed from the care of his mother. "Hence, for the well-being of my child, I commend my wife to be compliant and my brother to be more reasonable."

A SANCTUARY OF ART

BEETHOVEN did not exactly make it easy for his contemporaries to understand him and give him due acknowledgement, all the more so as each new work posed still more fresh problems and riddles. With the onset of total deafness, communication with him was restricted solely to the exchange of ideas or comments in his "conversation book." He was a man who would hear of no compromise, but insisted on a definite choice between whatever alternatives presented themselves. Willfulness, distrust and extravagance ruled his "worldly" existence, and his best friends had to make him see that his point of view was "not always compatible with a mean, miserable world." He was so hopelessly inexperienced in money matters that he even had to ask Oliva to explain terms like "to honor a bill." Despite the ample fees he must have been receiving at the time, he still found himself constrained to ask his publisher Steiner for a loan, which eventually amounted to three thousand florins—and that in a year which, in accordance with the contract, had brought him in over eight thousand florins. In the course of the next few years he was constantly asking for advances without satisfying the stipulated conditions. He complained repeatedly about dishonest servants and that he was constantly being robbed, and it does indeed seem that various people were illegally helping themselves on the quiet, knowing that it would not be noticed. We hear of him moving house, paying double rent, and being forever ready to help anyone in need, all of which contributed to the state of total mismanagement that was to become even worse in the years to come as a result of his insistence on saving every possible florin for the benefit of his nephew. Karl was at this point ten years old and, as might be anticipated, all his uncle's efforts on his behalf were in vain. The first plan to have him trained as an artist failed, and he himself then decided in turn to be a philologist, a businessman, and a soldier, sticking to the latter profession for a good five years. Later, when married and the father of a son and several daughters, he tried repeatedly and in vain to lay claim to the Beethoven estate. He died in 1858, though his branch of the family did not actually die out until 1917. For the purposes of this book only those aspects of Karl's life will be dealt with that directly increase our knowledge of his uncle's character and actions.

Though at first the child's mother was named as his guardian, Beethoven immediately began to contest the codicil to the will, insisting on "the total exclusion of the widow." In January he was then sworn in as Karl's sole guardian. Two weeks later he sent the boy to an institute run by a Herr Giannatasio del Rio, where he remained until 1819. Karl's mother then started an endless round of litigation which can be traced through a mass of documentation and statements. The whole business cast an unpleasant shadow over Beethoven's life for years until the widow's suit was definitively dismissed in July 1820.

His nomination as Karl's guardian did have one serious, undesirable side effect: it disrupted his work. Indeed he himself admitted on many occasions that excitement of any kind greatly hindered his creative process. The list of works composed during this difficult period bears out this statement fully. Hence we find no fewer than sixteen different openings for the song "Sehnsucht" of 1815/16, while among all the odds and ends produced in the first six months of the year only the song cycle *An die ferne Geliebte* shines out. From the summer months onwards he worked on the *Hammerklavier* Sonata op. 101, with which he felt he had created a "new world." 1817 produced one revision and the Quintet Fugue op. 137; 1818 saw without exception material of secondary quality, while 1819 resulted in the Piano Sonata op. 106 as well as the slow, tedious preparatory work on the Missa and the *Diabelli* Variations, both of which were begun in 1818/19 and not completed until 1823. It would, however, be mistaken to think that solely Karl obstructed his work tempo. This was also caused in part by the change of style which was then taking effect. A glance at the hundred or so letters and notes dated 1816 shows that they fall into five equal groups or categories. The first of these categories contains the letters addressed to Steiner and Haslinger which are continually concerned with financial demands; the second to the London Philharmonic Society, concerning money; the third deal with various household miseries; the fourth concern with the del Rio family with whom Karl was living. Only in the remaining letters does he rise above the worries of everyday life, writing to "his Leonora" (the singer, Anna Milder), to Countess Erdödy, and to the Brentanos in Frankfurt.

At times he indulged in puns, spiced with sarcasm, and often made up words. He once arranged a congratulatory canon for the del Rio household in such a way that after the words "May happiness and health fail you . . . ," the housewife was about to remark that this was no kind wish on his part, when he then added his final punch-line: ". . . never!" He pursued this game right into the last years of his life, and his conversation books abound in examples of exceeding vulgarity. He also commented on his own tricks in hastily noted aphorisms. In the same breath as the statement: "It is most difficult of all to acquire something from other people when you yourself appear to be a liar" he remarks: "Never allow people to be aware of the contempt they deserve, for you never know when you might need them." The same precept is applied in his dealings with publishers. For instance: "You reserve the right . . . to stipulate the date of publication, without the publishers in London and Germany knowing that the other exists, as they otherwise pay less, and it is unnecessary in any case. You can give the excuse that someone else has commissioned the work from you." Following this principle he had sent Charles Neate back to London with three already performed overtures instead of three new ones, as a result of which the Philharmonic Society told Neate "not to buy anything from Beethoven at all." Robert Birchall, Sir George Smart's co-publisher, considered these overtures so unimportant that he declared he would not publish them even if he were given them for nothing—and Neate had paid all of seventy-five guineas for them. Even Ferdinand Ries, Beethoven's friend and pupil, deemed one of them "unworthy of him." When Birchall took over four works for which a price had already been agreed on, Beethoven then demanded a further five pounds to cover copying and freight charges, and let many months go by before he sent the certificate of ownership necessary for publication. All in all, it is quite understandable that Birchall's successors were not interested in maintaining contact with Beethoven. From a list of his expenses dating from about this time it can be seen that of the three thousand, four hundred florins that he received under the stipulations of the decree, eleven hundred went on rent alone, nine hundred on servants' wages, and eleven hundred on Karl. In the light of this information we can understand his writing: "You must have capital . . . a farm property, then you can avoid this misery. In order to go on living and endure it all, a house in the suburbs; it is impossible to live in the country with Karl." He had once insinuated to his brother that whereas his life was very precious to him, he (Beethoven) would gladly lose his. It was equally indicative of his current situation when he wrote: "May all that is called life be sacrificed to the noble and the sublime—a sanctuary of art. Let me live, even if with help. If only such help could be found!"

He once excused himself to the Archduke for his failure to keep an appointment by saying that at precisely that moment he had had an inspiration for a chorus, and had thus rushed home to write it down; it had been a bad habit of his since childhood that he had to write down his inspirations immediately so that he did not forget them. The sketches he made that year include many that were never either taken up or developed, but also a great many ideas for the song cycle *An die ferne Geliebte.* Although he started work on these as soon as he "discovered" the texts, it is nevertheless believed that they are addressed to some specific figure in his life—perhaps Rahel Levin, who had attracted his attention back in Teplitz and who had been his secret inspiration ever since. He now forced himself to work every day from six in the morning until breakfast, and to spend his evenings looking through all he had written that day. Almost regretfully he admitted that "the precise coordination of several parts generally hinders the progress from one part to the next." Despite the fact that those near to him were of the opinion that his deafness had destroyed his feeling for tone, a closer study of his works themselves reveals just the opposite. The severe, extremely self-critical concentration apparent at this time is a direct result of his acknowledgement that "just as the state had to have a constitution, so also must each man have one for himself." He made notes of various analogies from the writings of Kant including: "order of the general laws of nature," "the concourse of atoms," "the advantageous arrangement of the structure"—all concepts which deal with proportion and strength in the same way he forces them together in his musical analogies. If we date the beginning of this new "third style" from the time of his work on the "Ertmann" sonata, it is definitely noticeable how much more concerned he became with the harmonizing of all the individual elements in the music. He then synchronized the climax of the melody with the metric structure, rhythmic expression, tonal development, and dynamic shading, without sacrificing the solid foundation of the form as a whole. The request he then received from Diabelli for a variation of his waltz came at the right moment to serve as a kind of testing ground for his ideas, though without in the least detracting from the exquisiteness of the cycle as a whole. Beethoven's art of interpretation and exposition and the multiplicity of idioms it embraced was claimed to represent all the fashionable styles of the day—Biedermeier, Empire, classic, and romantic—and is proof of the incomparable richness of his imagination and the innumerable methods of expression he had at his disposal. Following the age-old law that the will produces the technique most suited to it, Beethoven struggled to achieve even greater concentration of his composition. This he not unnaturally first set out to implement for his own instrument, the piano, though at the same time he was also working on both the *Missa solemnis* and the Ninth Symphony.

The world of his still perfect "inner ear" contrasted sharply to the wretched, vexating life he saw around him. The chief composition of the following year—1817/18—which he referred to as being "full of stress," was the Piano Sonata in B flat major op. 106, known as the *Hammerklavier*. Described by Robert Schumann as "the incomparably great" sonata, it in fact only became familiar in the concert hall through the performances of Franz Liszt. It was he who introduced it to the public in Paris, where it was admired among others by Richard Wagner, who held it to be literally without comparison. Is it based, as was suggested by Schering, on scenes from Schiller's *Jungfrau von Orleans?* A law unto itself, it is accessible only to those who genuinely seek it out.

As a result of a further devaluation of the currency, his

Beethoven, around 1818. Oil portrait by Ferdinand Schimon.

original salary had been reduced by forty florins to thirteen hundred and sixty florins in silver. Young Karl already knew just how to use the rivalry between his mother and his guardian to his own advantage, and behaved himself so impossibly that he had to be expelled from school. Whenever things became critical he would fly back to his mother, much to the despair of his helpless uncle. Not one of the available hearing aids was of any use to Beethoven anymore—not even Mälzel's, which he himself acknowledged to be the most effective. Verbal communication was thus no longer possible, but he seems to have retained some sense of proportion about the situation, as can be seen from the joke he is said to have made about the idea of a conversation between himself and Czerny's father, who was also almost stone deaf. His life continued along its usual ups and downs. During the winter he was in the city, and nearly always ill, while the summers were spent in the country, which agreed with both his health and temper. In the spring of 1816 the del Rio family met him in Baden with his face full of scratches after a quarrel with his servant. A year later he went first to Mödling, then to Heiligenstadt, and in the late autumn on to Nussdorf on the Danube. In 1818 he set off with all his baggage for Mödling again. But even here his life was still centered around his ward, Karl. He was a sensitive but capricious child, and we hear of him not being able to eat anything after he had been reprimanded—no doubt harshly, but with justification—"until he had cried himself out, otherwise the food would be poison to him." Considered by all to be an intelligent child, he lacked any trace of diligence or determination. He always had a thousand excuses at hand, and also knew full well that he could twist his uncle round his little finger. The latter was frequently in despair over the situation, and on occasion even wished he were dead. "I consider myself as good as lost. There is no other way out for me but to leave here; only by doing that can I once more soar to the heights of my art again. When I am here, I sink into the trivial things of life. Just one symphony, and then away, away, away! In the interim salaries have gone up, which could go on for years . . . So I can accomplish the great work for my poor nephew. Later on . . . wander through Italy and Sicily with some art-

The house where Beethoven spent the summers of 1818 and 1819.

ists." In 1818 he planned "to write a national anthem for the commemoration of the Battle of Leipzig in October which shall be performed each year. N.B. Each nation with its march and Te deum laudamus." His laments became more and more urgent as time went on: "O hear me, you ineffable one! Listen to me, the unluckiest of all mortals. I must once again sacrifice all the small joys of everyday life to my art." A letter of June 1817 written from Heiligenstadt to Countess Erdödy contains a detailed account of the intolerable conditions of his life; the fact that he had been ill continually since the previous October; that he sometimes suspected he was suffering from consumption; the hopeless state of his ears; and his worries about Karl. The prospect of being able to visit the Countess gives him fresh hopes of an improvement in his state of mind. But no mention whatever of his work. He was, nevertheless, still slaving away at the Scottish songs. During his stay in Mödling in the summer of 1819 he also composed eleven waltzes, minuets, and slow waltzes.

Quite possibly it was the letter he received from Ries in London, containing the commission for two symphonies for the London Philharmonic Society, that gave fresh impetus to his creative ability. Shortly before this the *Prometheus* Overture and the Eighth Symphony had been received with great enthusiasm at a charity concert organized by the Viennese lawyers. He was stimulated by any number of ambitious plans, but he did not in fact carry them out. Instead, he dabbled with some fugues, worked on piano sonatas that no one had requested, and experimented with song variations for piano with accompaniment. Only after completing the overture for the opening of the Josefstadt Theater did he set about weaving together the ideas and sketches that were to make up the Ninth Symphony.

A comparison of two portraits of him, such as those by Létronne and either Kloeber or Waldmüller, gives sufficient indication of the stage of development into which he had now passed. From this time on he was frequently to be seen in an extremely unkempt, disheveled state, especially at home, where he intentionally wore his very oldest clothes by way of an example to Karl—but in vain. His aristocratic intimate friends of earlier years were all dead; Brunswick had returned to live

1823. Portrait by Ferdinand Waldmüller.

on his estate; Zmeskall was also frequently ill; Gleichenstein had moved away; and Waldenstein had become rather distant. "I live almost alone in the greatest city in Germany." Some words of gratitude to E. T. A. Hoffman for his sympathy did not lead to any closer form of communication between the two men. The exchange of letters with friends in the Rhineland became more and more infrequent. Breuning was upset because his advice concerning Karl had been rejected out of hand. Even Oliva was affected, as he wrote in one of Beethoven's conversation books: "I was never actually infuriated by you, but I was sometimes hurt, because I did not deserve it." Hence he, too, only came when commanded. It almost seems as if Beethoven wished his friends to ferret him out and ask questions, but he barely heard them out before exploding: "Power which is united can overcome any numbers, no matter how great, that are not united . . . The bourgeoisie should be kept apart from nobler people, and I have become one of the latter. I am nothing, but even the nobility has more respect for me than I for it . . . For true art the mighty have no money . . ." Karl, who had in the meantime become Beethoven's "secretary," once counseled him: "Baron ———— is a chamberlain to the Kaiser. I mean, you shouldn't say anything against the government . . ." The same conversation books bear witness to many an agitation and emotional upset.

But complaints and accusations are not the only topics to appear. His love of good food, especially of delicacies, turns up frequently: "This inn is good only for those with a sweet tooth," "Austrian poems are like dumplings, like roast venison with raspberry sauce." His notes are scattered in a totally arbitrary fashion: "umbrella, boots, music, wine cellar, overcoat, country road, apartment with four rooms." They often deal with household affairs; over sixty notes addressed to his "Samaritan," as he called Frau Streicher, are concerned with one of the kitchen maids whom he accused of making a face when she had to carry in the firewood, although "Our Savior also had to carry His cross up to Calvary." He even noticed any cleaning rags that were missing. Such was the everyday world, the backdrop which he would have seen whenever he looked up from his sketch book. Hence his comment that "notes are more interesting than needs." He still had not found the suitable finale for the *Diabelli* Variations. The *Missa Solemnis,* which had long since been offered to the publishers, was still far from completion. The bagatelles of op. 119 take up some ideas he had originally thought out years before. The Piano Sonatas op. 110 and 111 dating from 1821 he could not bring himself to dedicate at all. But more than anything else he was intrigued by the commissions he had received in November 1822 to compose some quartets for Neate and the Russian Prince Galitzin. By the spring of 1823 the variations—a "masterpiece" according to Prince Galitzin—had progressed so far that, despite the fact that they had long since been promised to another publisher, they could be handed over to Diabelli. By the time the wearisome task of correction had been completed—delayed by a painful eye condition of Beethoven's—the publishers (Cappi-Diabelli-Peters) considered themselves "lucky to be able to open their list with the publication of a composition that is unique of its kind and . . . one that will remain so." In Leipzig, where no one knew what he was composing at the time, except for the Scottish songs and bagatelles, there was a general feeling that he seemed to have "dried up as far as larger works were concerned." To which he only laughed and retorted: "Just wait, I'll soon teach you another thing or two!" Among his friends there was much talk of the project for an oratorio that had been smoldering since 1815. Three years later when Hauschka asked him openly if he was ready to dedicate it to the Viennese Gesellschaft der Musikfreunde, he received the following reply ("I am ready, I am ready"):

Ich bin be-rei - - - t   ich bin be-rei - - - - t

137

It was probably not in the least annoying for him that Karl Bernard, who was commissioned to write the libretto, was extremely slow in completing his share. The subject matter Bernard had chosen—"The Victory of the Cross"—was the object of constant criticism from Beethoven, who used his objections as an excuse for postponing the composition again and again. It remained a favorite topic of conversation right to the end of his life, while he never actually did anything concrete about it.

The beginnings of the *Missa Solemnis* go back as far as the period of the litigation and trial concerning the guardianship of his nephew. The discussions about his nonaristocratic background, and the accusations of "exaggerated ideas and the use of inappropriate means of expressing them" so often leveled against him cannot exactly have contributed positively to his joy in creating. The first sketches for the *Missa* are to be found among those for the *Diabelli* Variations and the Piano Sonata op. 106 which date from the spring of 1819. Later that year, Schindler is said to have visited him in Mödling: "in a living-room with all the doors closed we heard the maestro sing, scream, and stamp his feet about everything from the fugue to the credo." After quite some time had passed Beethoven apparently opened the door and stood before the visitors looking extremely distressed. At first he could not speak coherently at all; finally he said: "A fine business. Everything gone wrong, and I haven't even eaten a bite since noon yesterday." Shortly after this Zelter also visited him in order to "see once more in this life the man who has done so much good . . . to bring about joy and edification." All he achieved was an accidental meeting on a country lane. Telling impressions of Beethoven are also to be found in the portraits by Ferdinand Schimon and Joseph Karl Stieler which date from the time of the composition of the *Missa Solemnis*.

Beethoven in 1819/20. Portrait by Joseph Karl Stieler.

At the beginning of 1820, he had won the court case over Karl, and still had the firm intention of handing over the completed *Missa* by the scheduled date; once the trial was out of the way, he was able once more to devote all his energies to his muse, and in rapid sequence composed the last three piano sonatas (op. 109 to op. 111). The first of these, the Sonata in E major, an "apotheosis of dance," is based on the most deeply impressive motifs: that in A major overflowing with feeling and goodness, with its perfectly balanced movements and intuitive penetration; and the third, in C minor, like an "enthronement of himself as the king of the realm of sound." Just how indescribable they are, and how impossible it is to translate them into the language of words, can be seen from the attempted interpretations of op. 109, which range from "sullen and temperamental" to "a miracle of grace, vitality and genius." According to one critic the last of these sonatas was "a long streak of lightning," for another "a nirvana," while for others it was like "the night with its mystery and its fear" or even "meditation." At the same time he was working on the *Missa* —though Archduke Rudolf's enthronement as Archbishop of Olmütz had long since been celebrated without it. The progress of the work was periodically held up by continued ill health. From 1820 on the *Missa* became the subject of intense speculations in the publishing world, in other worlds, long before the date of its completion could even be estimated.

Although Beethoven was just then considering buying a house in Mödling for which he had enough money in hand, he allowed himself to be dissuaded by Steiner. Instead, he moved no fewer than ten times in the course of the subsequent four years (including his customary summer visits to the country). After many attempts to find a solution to the problem, his nephew was finally placed in the institution run by Joseph Blöchinger, a pupil of Pestalozzi; Beethoven chose an apartment in the vicinity to be as close as possible to Karl. Despite the occasional disturbance by the boy's mother who even saw fit to bribe Beethoven's servants in order to see her child against his wishes, the household had become unrecognizably more orderly since the arrival of Anton Schindler—then only half Beethoven's age—to replace Oliva as his unpaid secretary, factotum and friend, being equally well-informed in business

Anton Schindler.

matters and music. He had first come to Beethoven's house six years previously while on an errand for another master, and had won the composer's sympathy through certain difficulties he encountered with the police in Brünn. While working in the office of Beethoven's legal adviser he gained an insight into the more personal aspects of the maestro he admired so greatly. He was also a violinist in one of the theater orchestras, and later became a conductor. In this latter capacity he persistently worked towards the popularization of Beethoven's creations. He soon knew Beethoven well enough to be able to admonish him not to be so indecisive, or to write: "Do not worry about the letters; all you need are your compositions, and the whole world rushes forward greedily to seize them!"

There can be no doubt that some of the things Schindler wrote were carelessly mistaken or misleading, and that his memory was frequently faulty. He was certainly highly over-estimated when selected in place of Rochlitz and Holz to write the first biography of the composer. One thing is definite, and that is that among those closest to Beethoven, there was a constant round of rivalry and intrigue, often taking advantage of his deafness. The only known picture of Schindler shows him as a careworn "tyrant" in his sixties, obsessed with the delusion that he alone had the right to lay down the law about the Beethoven tradition, but numerous notes written to him by Beethoven himself speak in his favor, as does the devoted loyalty with which he cared for his master through the most difficult period of his life. It may be unforgivable that he destroyed over 260 of the 400 recorded conversations which were in existence at the time of Beethoven's death, all the more so since he was clearly intelligent enough to be able to recognize their importance; but we should not forget that Beethoven's relationship with Schindler went through just as many ups and downs as did that with Oliva, or, for that matter, with his own brothers. It was undoubtedly no easy task to satisfy his constantly changing wishes and aims.

Schindler's appearance also coincided with that of his brother Johann, who had by then made enough money through his apothecary's business to buy himself an estate at Gneixendorf near Krems. During the winter he generally took rooms in the house in Vienna belonging to his in-laws where Beethoven also lived from time to time in later years. Like Karl he was held to be "talented, and somewhat conceited about the composer's fame." Devoid of any understanding for his brother's creations, he was able only to see the helplessness of his existence, and was genuinely concerned to advise him wherever possible to improve his situation. Hence he wrote into Beethoven's conversation book in 1822: "Rossini . . . became rich through his operas. I believe you too should write more operas." Beethoven himself, who addressed Johann alternately in terms of greatest endearment and outright hatred, finally proposed of his own volition that the latter should take over various works which he was to "barter off" on the publishers profitably. "In any case, as a businessman you are always a good counselor." The only thorns in his flesh were Johann's wife and her daughter, and he would have preferred Johann to leave them altogether and move in with him. Some of the derogatory things said about him are not to be taken literally, as for instance when he wrote to Ries in connection with the *Consecration of the House* Overture: "He bought it from me in order to make the fattest profit possible . . ."

Beethoven's own way of making a profit can be seen most clearly in the negotiations concerning the publication of the *Missa.* Having barely finished the first sketches for the work in mid-1819, he then offered the mass to Simrock in February of the following year, demanding in March an advance of one hundred louis d'or, followed later by one for two hundred

Nicolas Simrock. Lithograph by Weber.

ducats. Franz Brentano was engaged as mediator, and Simrock advanced a certain sum—but in German currency, which Beethoven refused to recognize. He already regretted having offered the mass so prematurely, and since he had received inquiries about it from several other sources, he thought of compensating Simrock in some other way. Two years later, however, the mass was still not finished; on the contrary, it had assumed proportions which even Beethoven himself did not care to anticipate. Indeed, one day he found himself admitting that this was his greatest work of all. In the meantime it had been offered to Peters, Schlesinger, Artaria, Steiner, and Diabelli in turn, in the hopes of obtaining a higher fee, and the price had already risen to one thousand florins. Beethoven had earlier offered his brother a few works in receipt of an advance payment, to get himself out of a "tight spot" or two, the understanding at the time being that Johann had full rights over the works in question, and he was then able to use these rights as a refuge from the pressing demands of the publishers. At one point there was even talk of further masses he would like to compose. In March 1823 the Archduke finally held his copy of the mass in his hands. A temporary disagreement with Johann led to the decision not to have the mass printed, but to offer it only in handwritten copies at fifty ducats each to the wealthy aristocrats. By mid-1823 offers to this effect had been sent to most of the German princes, as well as to Tuscany and Paris, mostly via the embassies there, and Beethoven personally wrote to various influential personalities, such as Goethe, Cherubini, Spohr, and Zelter. But all the effort resulted in only ten acceptances. There was no reply at all from Weimar, which more than upset Beethoven, who could of course not know that the seventy-four-year-old poet was extremely ill and not far from death's door. Despite the fact that in some of the letters he categorically stated that the mass would not be published—"at least for the time being," he wrote Goethe—in the following year he drew up an agreement with the Mainz publisher Bernhard Schott. A subscription offer made through the publishers in 1825 brought in two hundred and ten advance orders. Delivery of the manuscript—three volumes containing four hundred and forty pages—dragged on until January 1825. The last sheets went to press in March 1827, and the completed work "left the press at almost the same time as the death of the incomparable composer," as was stated in the announcement heralding the appearance of the *Missa*. "It is a work for eternity!" he had written in his conversation book in February 1823.

Diverse original comments, often scribbled in the margin of his sketches or incorporated in the text of his letters, give only a vague idea of what was stimulating his mind in the course of the three and a half years that he spent working on this "greatest and most admirable" of creations. A sentence of his handed down by his violinist friend, Karl Holz, gives some indication: "Writing a fugue is no art; I composed them by the dozen while I was a student. But the imagination also has to stake its claims, and nowadays a truly poetic element must be introduced into the traditional form." Visitors described his method of working as follows: "He always has a little notebook at hand . . . and in it he takes down every musical idea as it occurs to him, regardless of the fact that the pages are un-lined . . . He alone holds in his memory the thread with which he then turns this maze of dots and circles into the richest and most admirable of harmonies . . . He seems to hear only with the inner ear . . ." Rochlitz quotes some significant admissions made by Beethoven himself: "For some time now I have not found it easy to write. I sit and think and think for ages before I am actually able to put it to paper . . . once I get going, it's all right . . ." The actor Heinrich Anschütz observed him "engraving mystical inscriptions onto a piece of paper," at the same time drumming with his fingers on the table. Louis Schlösser, who was delegated to inform him of the advance order for the *Missa* placed by his former master in Hesse, jotted down the following verbatim statements immediately after his conversation with Beethoven: "I carry my thoughts about with me for a long time, before I write them down. Meanwhile my memory is so tenacious that I am sure never to forget, not even in years, a theme that has once occurred to me. I change things, discard, and try again until I am satisfied. Then, how-ever, there begins in my head the development in every direc-tion and, since I know exactly what I want, the fundamental idea never deserts me—it arises before me, it grows—I see and hear the picture in all its extent and dimensions before my mind like a cast, and there remains for me nothing but the task of writing it down, which is quickly accomplished when I have the time, for I sometimes take up other work, but never to the confusion of one with the other. You will ask me where I get my ideas from. I cannot say for certain. They come uncalled, sometimes directly, and sometimes in association with other things. It is as if I could wrest them with my own hands from Nature herself, in the woods, on walks, in the silence of the night, in the early morning, stirred into being by moods which the poet would translate into words, but which I put into sounds; and these go through my head ringing, humming and storming until at last I have them before me as notes." In this respect it is interesting to read the comments made by Schubert: "That is his way: he usually makes a note of his ideas for various melodies, more often than not in words, with no more than a few odd notes of music thrown in . . . For him art has already become a science. He knows what he is capable of, and his imagination simply obeys his unfathomable powers of reflection . . . He can do anything, but we are not yet able to understand everything, and a lot of water will flow under the bridge before the world in general is able to understand him . . . Nobody can really comprehend Beethoven fully; to do so one must be highly intelligent, extremely emotional, and involved in a terribly unhappy love affair, or in some other way unhappy."

But he could also be seen in "a more natural and happy" mood, when he would crack one joke after the other, and was "full of exciting combinations and paradoxes." "The man who brings sheer joy to millions," as Rochlitz put it. At about this time Johann arranged a meeting between Beethoven and Rossini, who professed as much praise for Beethoven's quartets as the latter did for Rossini's lighthearted talent, which had just then been so overwhelmingly acclaimed by the Viennese. About this time, too, Schubert handed over a copy of his *Variations on a French Song* which he had dedicated to Beethoven. The two men were undoubtedly far closer to each other than the surviving documentary evidence makes clear. Schubert seems to have withheld even from Schindler his difficult conversations with Beethoven, and the fact that he understood the latter's strange individuality.

The period preceding the publication of the *Diabelli* Variations, the *Missa Solemnis* and the great Piano Sonata op. 111 was occupied with a variety of incidental pieces, including the first version of the "Opferlied" op. 121b, the "Bundeslied" op. 122, and some contributions for the festival play *Die Weihe des Hauses* (The Consecration of the House) which was staged to mark the opening of the Josefstadt Theater under the direction of Hensler, of whom he had a high opinion and to whom he then shortly afterwards dedicated a congratulatory minuet for orchestra by way of a birthday gift.

Of the *The Consecration of the House* Overture it is sufficient to say that it is completely out of the ordinary, crystallizing a theme of Bach-like clarity endowed with the brilliance of Handel. That same year Beethoven decided he wanted to assist Ignaz Umlauf with the revival of *Fidelio,* but the project collapsed even before rehearsals had come to an end. Beethoven laid all the blame on his deafness and in secret sought medical help one last time for his left ear, which was the less defective of the two. His brother even offered a reward of ten thousand ducats "to the physician who cures him." Beethoven's doctor, Dr. Smetana, was no doubt well aware that there was no point in harboring any illusions, and probably said so. Another course of treatment at the hands of the medically skilled Father Weiss involved injections of oil which momentarily relieved the pain but could not effect a complete cure, so that he discontinued the treatment: as his sketch books demonstrated, he had been seized by a new wave of creative fever.

I STILL HOPE TO BRING A FEW MORE GREAT WORKS INTO THE WORLD

THE delivery of the *Diabelli* Variations, the new overtures and the last three piano sonatas marked the close of a period of immense mental activity. Once again he felt the temptation to write another opera, prompted not only by his brother, but equally by Count Moritz Lichnowsky. Various themes were mentioned. The oratorio plan was also broached again and Karl Bernard was commissioned to alter it, or make some fresh suggestions. Beethoven was clearly disturbed by all the indecision: "I am not going to write what would give me most pleasure, but what will bring in the most money, which I need badly. This does not necessarily mean that I write solely for the money —as soon as this period is behind me I hope to write on that highest of all artistic themes, *Faust*." In order to get the composition under way as soon as possible, Johann again suggested that Beethoven should go down to his country estate with him in May and set to work immediately on the opera.

Visitors at this time showered him with compliments: "Each of your compositions has its own character"; "A friend from London wrote me that 'Beethoven is the god of music' "; "You are worshipped, because your music is religion." Grillparzer naïvely enquired whether Beethoven was never going to marry, although he himself hallowed the view that "women with minds have no bodies, and those with bodies have no minds." Dr.

Bach comforted him: "Marriage is the highest form of luck and happiness so long as one has made the right choice; but it is hell if one makes the wrong choice." Even his nephew Karl had enough savoir-faire despite his seventeen years to add: "As a German author once said, the ancients were quite right to incorporate not only the three graces, but also the three furies within the female form." A mention of Count Gallenberg caused Beethoven to say of the latter's wife, the former Giulietta Guiccidardi: "J'étais bien aimé d'elle . . .," but he added: ". . . if I had wanted to spend all my vital energy like *that,* what would have been left for better, nobler things?"

From the confusion of entries in his conversation books in

Giulietta Guicciardi. Anonymous miniature.

the spring of 1823 we can follow his preoccupation with the Grillparzer text for *Melusine,* which resulted in the poet visiting him on a number of occasions. In April he received a visit from the twelve-year-old Franz Liszt who hoped to persuade him to attend a concert at which he was to perform; the visit is recorded in the boy's somewhat clumsy entry in Beethoven's conversation book in which he says how happy he is to have been able to make the elder composer's acquaintance. His next visitor was a baron who agreed to rent Beethoven his villa at Hetzendorf for the summer. He, Johann, and Karl moved there together, and Beethoven described the place as "a true paradise." Soon, however, the master of the house tired of bestowing favors, so that Beethoven had to move, with Schindler's help, to Baden. There, however, his former landlord was only prepared to take him in again on the condition that he replace the window shutters he had covered with notes and sketches the previous year, which had subsequently been sold as "souvenirs" to summer visitors. In addition to his catarrh and bowel troubles he had also in the meantime acquired a tiresome eye infection, which caused him endless difficulties over the correction of the *Missa* score. During the absence of his brother and nephew his days were occupied with bathing, walking, various encounters, and work on the new symphony. His most noteworthy visitor was Carl Maria von Weber, whom he greeted with open joy.

Just how extensive his preparations for the Ninth Symphony were can be seen from the fact that sketches for it were strewn in among those for the Eighth a full ten years earlier. Yet although the intention to set Schiller's "Ode to Joy" to music dates back to Bonn days, as the poet himself learned, the actual process of its creation up to 1823 can only be traced through various allusions Beethoven made in his writings. The plan for an "adagio cantique" dates from about 1818. Into the final form he worked the two symphony schemes of "a pious song within a symphony in the old mode" and an "allegro in praise of Bacchus." Beethoven reached complete fulfillment in both this symphony and the *Missa Solemnis*. The *Missa* also expanded far beyond its original purpose as an "occasional piece," and finally outgrew the limitations of the person, place and occasion for which it was originally intended. From being a testimony to one specific man's faith it succeeded in becoming a seemingly timeless allegory of religious feeling, removed from the bounds of denominational restrictions. When, some time later, the authorities declared that the music of Haydn, Mozart, and Beethoven were not suitable for liturgical purposes, the *Missa* was in no way demoted, but rather acquired the transcendental, unparalleled significance that it still possesses today. Nietzsche's opinion that its author had "composed music about music," and that the use of texts—even the Schillerian ode in the last movement of the Ninth—marked a decline in Beethoven's genius, is almost identical with Wagner's comment that the *Missa* was a "purely symphonic work, Beethoven at his truest."

Since the censor forbade the performance of a mass within the framework of a public concert, Beethoven had to get round the ruling by selecting three parts—the "Kyrie," "Credo," and "Agnus Dei"—which he described in the program as hymns. Thus it was that they were heard for the first time, together with the *Consecration of the House* Overture and the Ninth Symphony, on May 7, 1824. Out of annoyance at the "big fuss" being made over Rossini by the Viennese, he decided to stage the first performance of his new works in Berlin; but when his friends came to hear of this plan, they got together and made him promise not to deprive them of the première of "his latest masterpieces." Although they achieved their aim, there were still the normal difficulties involved with organizing a concert,

Drawing by Stefan Dekker, 1824.

including the high cost of renting a hall, and the constant rivalry about who should play and conduct. Unusually steep overheads decimated the net profit to such an extent that Beethoven actually fainted on hearing the amount cleared when all the necessary payments had been made. Nevertheless, despite insufficient rehearsals the concert was greeted with greater storms of applause than ever before. A repeat performance two weeks later even made a loss. Most startled of all were the musical experts, who had expected that after ten years of deafness Beethoven would only be able to produce dry, abstract compositions entirely lacking in imagination, yet his new symphony breathed as much fresh, vital, even youthful spirit, as much power, novelty, and beauty as had ever come from this most original of men. The following year, when Ries successfully led a performance of the Ninth Symphony with four hundred and twenty-two players at the Lower Rhine Music Festival, he acknowledged to his old master that it was a work without parallel, and that had he composed nothing but this symphony, he would still have become immortal.

Beethoven's everyday existence continued to be dominated by numerous worries which he made no attempt to conceal. He was oppressed by the fact that he owed money to Brentano, Simrock, and Steiner. He wrote to his legal adviser that death might come at any time, and wanted to have his will drawn up. His chronic abdominal and catarrhal conditions had of late led him to fear that "the thread of life might soon be severed," or that he might be struck down suddenly just like his grandfather had been. He nevertheless continued to hope in "Apollo and the Muses," saying that he still owed them so much, that his brain was still flowing with inspiration which demanded to be realized. Shortly after these two concerts he departed for the country again, this time to Penzing. But his whereabouts rapidly became known, and he had to retire to the castle of Guttenbrunn near Baden in order to escape from the staring eyes of curious onlookers. Karl, who lived with him only part of the time, was the target for numerous reproaches. At about this time Streicher suggested that Beethoven should organize a series of six subscription concerts each year, as well as the publication of a complete edition of his works. However, any number of similar projects had been suggested since the time of the first performance of *Fidelio* in 1805, but none of them had ever come to fruition.

Again and again he was sought out by curious visitors and travelers, who later—most after his death—reported their conversations with him, based either on faulty memories of the occasion or, worse still, on complete fabrication. Perhaps the most important visitors of that year were Louis Schlösser, the writer J. Sporschil, the Englishman E. Schulz, Carl Maria von Weber and Franz Liszt. That year he did not return to Vienna until the beginning of November, and very soon afterwards had to move again to avoid the stormy scenes with Karl, and because the neighbors had complained about his loud piano-playing. It was in this next sparse, uncomfortable apartment that he received the invitation of the London Philharmonic Society to come to London, on the most favorable of conditions, the following February. Indecision, the extra charge he claimed for traveling expenses and his bad health all worked to reduce this plan, like all the others, to nothing. Soon after the publication of the *Missa Solemnis* Schott received the String Quartet op. 127, which had already been performed by Schippanzigh, but unfortunately without any success. The quartet only reaped public approval and moderate understanding when it was interpreted subsequently by the more sensitive violinist, Joseph Böhm. Beethoven seems at this time to have devoted more of his energies than usual to the composition of incidental canons and contributions to commemorative albums. Ideas for these pieces are to be found even among the sketches for the next string quartets, together with comments that do not appear to have anything to do with the quartets themselves.

No one who has heard Beethoven's last five quartets could fail to be impressed by their uniqueness. Heimeran described them as "the most precious, imperishable possession of quartet playing." No matter how confused some of the phrases may appear on paper, a fact which consequently places them beyond the scope of most amateur quartets, closer inspection reveals a simple central motif, playfully loose and enticing, like the theme of the first phrases of the allegro of op. 127:

Despite the rapid succession in which these five "giant" quartets were composed, extending for the most part over no more than two years, the complete individuality of each single work is nothing short of astonishing. One can only begin to appreciate their abstract qualities by examining the degree of compositional purity, the perfection with which the various ideas are interwoven, and the fact that their substance defies all definition, for they "confound utterly any distinctness, indeed the entire realm of empirical reality" (Nietzsche). The only other works to come anywhere near them in quality are Schubert's great opus in G major and his Quintet op. 163, which are no less "classical" than any works of Beethoven; and, as if out of another world altogether, the last compositions of Haydn and Mozart, which, though in a completely different style, are equally faultless and praiseworthy. It is possible that Beethoven was once again inspired by poetry. Schering suggests he may have been inspired by *The Merry Wives of Windsor, A Midsummer's Night Dream, Hamlet,* and (for the last of all)

Faust. Of far greater significance would seem to be the fact that even Böhm found himself having to repeat the very same evening the quartet—probably op. 127—that he had just introduced to the public for the first time. Only in this way, by repeated hearing and personal involvement can the listener experience the full emotional impact of this deeply personal work. It is inconceivable that the inherent activating power and distinct symbolism of these quartets should not affect all who hear them. For those, however, who cannot at first come to terms with them, it may be a comfort to know that almost all those—from university professors to amateur music lovers—who heard the first performance of op. 127 in 1825 admitted that they had understood "little or nothing at all of the development of the composition . . ."

At the same time Beethoven produced occasional pieces almost as if they were donations for the poor: two waltzes and an écossaise for the benefit of a needy actor, who was given permission to have them published; and a number of canons, some of them as yet not "deciphered," such as *Ich war hier, Doktor* for Dr. Braunhofer. By composing playful combinations of notes he tried to overcome his concern that he was gradually losing the fierce determination "to make his spirit prevail at all costs" which had been the guiding principle of his entire life for the past thirty years. The inflammation of the bowels plagued him until May 1825, when he was driven to take a course of treatment in Baden. Karl had in the meantime become a student at the polytechnic institute. Beethoven's relationship with Haslinger had been upset by the latter's oversensitive reaction to a rather crude joke, and he himself had broken with Schindler. At first the gap was filled by the stimulus of various new encounters. These visits sometimes led to extended drinking bouts, to the extent that Beethoven on one occasion was not even sure what "filth" he had written the day before, although he had probably just been amused by some catchy line or other.

According to one anecdote handed down about his stay in Baden, he is supposed to have had his hat blown off by the wind one day while going for a walk; at first he apparently chased it, but was then distracted by something more interesting. Oblivious of everything, he went on walking until some hours later he attracted the suspicion of the village policeman who arrested him. His assertion that he was Beethoven brought him nothing but a shower of derision on the part of the policeman, who declared that Beethoven could not possibly look like he

Beethoven's last residence, the "Schwarzspanierhaus" in Vienna.

did, and that he was far more likely a plain ragamuffin. Beethoven had to wait for hours, complaining fiercely, before a music teacher living in the village was brought along to relieve him from the awkward situation. He then spent the night at the music teacher's house before returning to Baden the next day in the mayor's ceremonial carriage. From Baden he then wrote asking Johann to join him. In order to persuade his brother to come, he played on the animosity between the latter and Schindler, saying that if Johann did not come, he would be forced to rely on Schindler. "I'd really rather give Mr. Shitler a Viennese hand-kiss and send him off . . . If I have to have someone around me, my brother is the one for the position." On his brother's refusal, he next turned to Holz, who was invited to appear the following Friday. His quiet, reliable manner must have been greatly welcome as a counteraction to Beethoven's increasing feeling of depression. In Holz, he felt he had found someone who spoke the same language as himself.

The highpoint of his social life during this period was formed by the concerts held before a small, intimate group of friends in a Viennese hotel in the middle of September. The Schuppanzigh ensemble played again and again the Quartet in A minor and the last piano trio, after which Beethoven himself improvised freely. Schlesinger, to whom the new work was bequeathed, invited the whole audience to a sumptuous banquet which extended into a long drinking session. Those present included, at long last, Sir George Smart from London, and the cloth-merchant, Johann Wolfmayer, who was a close friend of Beethoven. Among the women there was one of Leopold Kozeluch's daughters, a widowed singer, whom Schlesinger claimed Beethoven wanted to marry. Smart then accompanied Beethoven back to Baden, where they indulged in more dining and wining, and Smart presented him with a diamond pin. Only in mid-October did Beethoven feel the urge to return to Vienna, where he took an apartment not far from the Breunings, in the "House of the Black Spaniard." This was to be his last dwelling. There had just been a round of fresh trouble over his nephew, who had suddenly disappeared, and was presumably with his mother. Having previously bombarded the youth with complaints and accusations, his tone then changed to one of utmost affection: "I promise you, there will be no reproaches . . . I embrace you a thousand times . . . my son who is not lost, but reborn." Karl was then sent to lodge with a family near the institute at which he was studying. Beethoven, meanwhile, was already working on the String Quartet op. 130 for Prince Galitzin, which he completed in November.

Despite an apparent interim recovery, medical treatment nevertheless remained necessary. Even before his journey to Baden Dr. Braunhofer had received the following letter written in dialogue form: "(Doctor): How are you, my patient?—(Patient): We are still rather poorly—I should like to be able to sit at my writing desk again and feel a little stronger . . ." A short canon which he added as a postscript expressed the hope that his doctor would be able to "keep the bars on the door of death":

Dok-tor sperrt das Tor dem Tod. No-te hilft auch aus der Not.

Dok-tor sperrt das Tor dem Tod. No-te hilft auch aus der Not.

Then in February 1826 we find him beginning a sentence to Karl: "But this is the last year . . ." Dr. Braunhofer had to be sent for frequently, and he ordered Beethoven not to drink wine or coffee, and only to eat the diet prescribed by him. Beethoven did not let any consideration of his health prevent him from making plans for further concerts, though the only one to actually take place was a performance of op. 130 by Schuppanzigh, at which "every single lover of quartet music to be found in Vienna" was present. Both the presto and the danza were applauded so enthusiastically that they had to be played again, while the fugue was thought to be too long and incomprehensible. Only when pressed to it later by Artaria did Beethoven consent to replace it by a new movement. With respect to the many complex runs which could throw even the best lead violinist off key, Schuppanzigh is reputed to have earned himself the rebuke: "Does he believe that I think of his miserable violin when I feel the inspiration to compose?" Beethoven's personal favorite among the movements is supposed to have been the cavatina, which he himself could not hear without being moved to tears. It is this movement that contains the strangely disquieting part marked "oppressive" which some critics have without any justification assumed to be a reference to a heart attack Beethoven may possibly have suffered. However, at no point was a heart condition ever mentioned among his ailments. The quartet had not even been performed once before he was already working on a new quartet in C sharp minor, possibly intended for Charles Neate. It consists of one vast movement in seven parts without a break. Never since have any themes been treated with such complexity and diversity as here, and it cannot be a coincidence that the Great Fugue is quoted almost literally in the "ritmo di tre battute." When Beethoven was already bedridden, young Gerhard von Breuning—Stephan's son—once wrote with youthful carelessness on his conversation pad that the quartet of his played the day before by Schuppanzigh had not been well received, and the older man wrote curtly: "They'll like it soon enough!" The quartet in question was probably either the one in C sharp minor just referred to or else the last quartet he completed, the op. 135 in F major.

His contacts with the outside world became more and more

tenuous and unreal. The violinist, Karl Holz, recorded Beethoven as saying to him: "You will notice a new manner of voice-treatment, and, thank God, there is less lack of imagination than ever before!" One last time he debated the possibility of carrying out some of the unrealized projects of earlier years; with Karl Bernard he discussed the theme of "The Triumph of the Cross," with Kuffner "The Elements" and "Saul." Johann Wolfmayer had already paid him an advance of one thousand florins for the requiem he had been promised. Grillparzer's *Melusine* was still not completed, although Goethe's *Claudine* or *Faust* lay much closer to his heart. His sketch books contain ideas for a tenth symphony which he had already thought out fully in his head.

Beethoven's physician now advised him to go to a spa with more invigorating water; Ischl and Gastein were mentioned, but his wavering indecision had become worse still as a result of further disagreements with Karl, in the course of which they even came to blows. Beethoven even wrote to his nephew imploring him not to do anything that might in any way precipitate his death. But in fact it was Karl who was closer to this phenomenon; his attempt to drown himself was thwarted by Holz, and his landlord removed the pistol and ammunition he had in his possession. His next move was to sell his watch in order to buy two pistols, with which he tried to shoot himself at the end of July in the ruins of Rauhenstein near Baden. The first shot missed totally, and the second merely wounded him on the temple. He was discovered by a passing carter who drove him home to his mother. The shock experienced by his uncle, who was immediately informed, can easily be imagined. Karl's wound was treated, and although he was in no danger of dying, he had to be put into hospital until he recovered. The local vicar was instructed by the police to see to the boy's spiritual state—suicide was a crime under Austrian law. He finally received his uncle's permission to enter the army, and with Breuning's assistance was accepted as a cadet in one of Baron von Stutterheim's regiments. In gratitude for this service, Beethoven dedicated his highly praised quartet, op. 131, to the Baron instead of his friend Wolfmayer. In order to prevent any further troubles, he then took Karl with him down to his brother's estate at Gneixendorf at the end of September. While his nephew's wound was being treated, he wandered through the fields humming to himself and taking notes as he went. The people of the neighborhood thought he was quite mad, and legend has it that even the oxen were frightened by his gesticulations. Gradually the rancor subsided, and he regained a shade of his former good humor. If he allowed his muse "to fall asleep," it was only "so that she'll wake up all the more refreshed." He requested Haslinger to send him some of the fees due to him as "it is unfortunately not a matter of indifference whether we have any money or not." He then sketched a new finale for op. 130 to replace the Great Fugue, and wrote it into its final form in the course of October and November.

Gneixendorf being an extremely unsuitable place for him to spend the winter, Johann pressed him to return to Vienna. The fateful journey was made on an open farm wagon so that they arrived frozen to the bone at the village inn en route where they had to spend the night in an unheated room. Beethoven was seized by a feverish chill accompanied by coughing and a stitch in his side. In a state of utter exhaustion he finally reached his apartment in Vienna. Due to misunderstandings no one called a doctor immediately. He himself finally sent for Holz who summoned Professor Wawruch, who treated him initially for acute pneumonia. For some unknown reason his usual doctors, Braunhofer and Straudenheim, were not available at the time. After a temporary improvement he then suffered a relapse as a result of which his basic ailment—originally diagnosed as dropsy— flamed up and was rediagnosed as cirrhosis of the liver. Karl had still not joined his regiment, but was idling away the time with drinking and gambling. Holz, who had recently married, was replaced once more by Schindler, who did everything in his power to relieve the suffering of his fatally ill friend.

Wawruch soon had cause to be alarmed when the expected improvement failed to materialize, and the patient succumbed instead to jaundice and diarrhea, accompanied by nightly choking fits and severe edema. But Beethoven did not give up all hope, and despite his weakness managed to dictate letters and even to compose the first 24 measures of a string quintet in C major. Household problems continued to upset him from time to time, as when he had to dismiss one of the servants because of dishonesty. Many of his neighbors and friends stepped in to help him in any way they could. Von Breuning, himself an ill man, sent his son, and Frau Streicher and Baron Pasqualati vied with one another for the honor of looking after him.

After Karl's departure for the regiment at the turn of the year Beethoven's entire life centered around the letters he received from his nephew; whenever no post arrived for a few days he would be consumed with worry. Dr. Malfatti was also summoned and for a short while Beethoven thought that the iced punch he prescribed was going to be the answer to his problems. But respite proved to be only temporary, and repeated surgery was necessary to remove the fluid that had accumulated in his body. The hopelessness of his condition was soon all too clear to those close to him. In February he wrote to his London friends, Stumpff, Moscheles, and Smart, as a result of which he received an immediate advance of one hundred pounds on a benefit concert to be held on his behalf. He saw various visitors to Vienna, and those who came to see him included Schubert, Count Lichnowsky, Gleichenstein, Diabelli, and Holz. Johann Wolfmayer was in tears as he parted from his old friend.

As late as March he wrote promising Moscheles the delivery of a symphony which he described as "lying already in sketch form on my desk." In December he had written to Wegeler: "I still hope to bring a few more great works into the world, and then I can bring my career to a close." As things turned out, his last composition was a canon for Holz set to Lichtenberg's profound epigram: "We all err, but each one of us errs differently."

The doctors eventually gave up all hope of curing him, and merely prescribed that he should be allowed to have anything he pleased. At Beethoven's request Schott sent him a cask of 1806 Rüdesheimer wine, and Pasqualati responded similarly with champagne and game. Johann Hummel and Ferdinand von Hiller were among the last witnesses to his rapidly deteriorating condition. By March 23 he was "weak and pitiful, unable to utter anything but an occasional sigh." They managed to get him to sign the codicil to his will confirming that Karl was to be his sole legatee, but that the capital of his estate was to fall only to his natural or testamentary heirs. The capital in question amounted to ten thousand ducats. Wawruch sent for a priest, and none of his intimate friends present could subsequently agree as to whether his words: "Plaudite, amici, comoedia finita est" were in fact said before or after the priest's visit. On the evening of March 24 he began his final struggle with death. He died at about six o'clock on March 26, while a thunderstorm was raging over Vienna, and his eyes were closed by Anselm Hüttenbrenner, a pupil of Salieri and a friend of Schubert. His last completed composition, the finale which he wrote for the Great Fugue of op. 130, seems to have the air of a "dance of death":

165

According to Gustav Nottebohm, at least fifty symphonies could have been composed from the unused ideas and sketches Beethoven left behind. He took up the thought of the canon *Es muss sein* (It must be) again in the quartet for Wolfmayer, turning it into a question: "Must it be?" This very question could well have been the thought in the minds of all music lovers when Beethoven's troubles with his ward and the distressing details of his illness became public knowledge.

It remains only to say a word about his funeral. About twenty

Beethoven's coffin being carried into the Holy Trinity Church, Vienna, to be blessed. Sepia drawing by Franz Xaver Stöber.

thousand people accompanied his coffin from his house to the cemetery at Währing, among them Franz Schubert bearing a burning candle. He was buried to the sound of his own equali— the ones composed in Linz, arranged for voices—and Mozart's *Requiem*. Cherubini's *Requiem* was played at the memorial service held two days later in the Karlskirche, and it very probably aroused emotions similar to those which had caused Beethoven himself to cry out at his brother's funeral: "Cast your eyes down, my dear brother! Yes, I have mourned you and mourn you still ..."

THUS THE PAST
BRINGS FORTH THE PRESENT*

BEETHOVEN himself gave an indication of his place in history when he said that he expected nothing more than to have his name added to those of Handel, Bach, Gluck, Mozart, and Haydn. The fact that he considered Cherubini to be the greatest composer of his time, and felt that from 1822 onwards he himself was overshadowed by Rossini, makes it evident that he was unaware of both the turn of the times and his own role as the innovator of a new era—one that has lasted up to the present day.

The careers of the four greatest composers Vienna ever produced—Haydn, Mozart, Beethoven, and Schubert—followed so closely on each other that it is all too easy to overlook the fact that they belonged to four different generations. Hadyn completed his training and wrote his first string quartet in the same year that

* Line from Beethoven's notebook, 1815.

Mozart was born; at the time of Beethoven's baptism the "concertmaster of Salzburg" was already composing his fourth operetta; and while Schubert was struggling over his first attempts at composition, Beethoven had already completed all but the Ninth Symphony. Although none of the four was a native Viennese, the "Viennese Classical School" rose around them—though no other common characteristics can be named beyond "simplicity, clarity, and conciseness." Despite the prevailing overvaluation of structure—the claim that "the spirit of music is to be found in the form"—it has long been proved that very different forces were responsible for the expansion of the "one-dimensional" form as practiced by Vivaldi and Corelli into the "two-dimensional" form of the Mannheim School, which then became the "Sonata style" of the Viennese masters without undergoing any radical change.

All the more food for thought is provided by the fact that we still refer to the all music of the two hundred years preceding Beethoven, from Jacopo Peri's *Dafne* almost up to the *Magic Flute,* under the blanket term "Baroque." In contrast, there is a profusion of term for every nuance of style that appeared in the course of Beethoven's era, from Rococo and Sentimentality through Louis Seize, pre-, early, and high Classicism, Empire, Neo-Gothic, and Biedermeier, right up to all the variations of Romanticism. They are witness to nothing but the openly agitated mood that effected the transition of artistic patronage from the hands of the aristocracy to those of the bourgeoisie, a phenomenon brought about ultimately by one single event—the French Revolution. It would be inconceivable to think of Hadyn throwing himself into the fray; Mozart's *Figaro* seems very remote from any political outlook; and Schubert's words revealed no sympathy for the advocates of human rights. Beethoven alone was swept up wholeheartedly by enthusiasm for the principles of the Revolution. He could not help but be fired by those ideas of humanity, nationalism, and the true dignity of man, and by their pioneer, Bonaparte, whom he admired so greatly. When the phenomenon that he had taken as a signal of better things to come exposed itself as nothing more than a phantom, he was so deeply disappointed that he withdrew to "the realm of the mind, the dearest of all monarchies." The dissolution of the numerous small ecclesiastical and secular courts led to the disbandment of their orchestras, and the many musicians had to find employment in the newly founded theaters, municipal orchestras, and schools of music, which in turn brought about the establishment of a new tradition: the public concert.

In Vienna, however, things were slow to change, probably because of the continued patronage of the imperial court. Indeed, Beethoven was scarcely "plunged into freedom" by the death of the Archduke when he was bound anew to the royal family, this time for life. Since his family and teachers were not able to give him much more than the "skill to create musical skeletons," there can be no doubt that the musical climate of Vienna contributed substantially to his development. But his highly individual, "wholly incomprehensible" quality was something that evolved exclusively out of his innermost being. Now, as then, we can testify to the validity of the statement in his own hand which stood framed on his writing desk: "No mortal has ever raised the veil of my mind."

Up to this time Beethoven, as his grandfather and father before him, had contended chiefly with the overhaul of the musical tradition dictated by "progress in the world of art." Hence we find a contemporary critic writing in the year of the *Fidelio* premiere that "the more light-hearted piano music of such composers as Pleyel, Wanhal, and Kozeluch is completely out of fashion." At that point Beethoven had already published nearly one hundred pieces, including no fewer than twenty piano sonatas, so that it is not difficult to guess what had "swept away the "light-hearted piano music." For the first time in the history of music we find a repertoire that fuses new and rediscovered older works in an exciting program that does not lose its immediacy from one generation to the next. Not by any means have all the works of those days survived up to the present; nevertheless, the music lover of the twentieth century is able to choose from a vast repertoire embracing two thousand years of musical creation and ranging from the pre-Christian songs of the Seikilos to the latest eccentric experiments with sounds, and he is asked to judge a range of music from Bach to Bartok. To this day music is still said to "seize hold of the best" and is yet also said to be "the most relentless of the arts in conjuring up the past"; indeed, according to Karl Jaspers, "the very essence of its effect" depends on this quality.

We need no further proof of the tremendous influence of the four Viennese masters on the musical world of today. Though our ears are now trained to new and bolder things, the statement still holds true that "the secondary work of the great artist is more important to us than the major work of the inferior artist" (Albert Einstein). If we put aside those works which Beethoven himself described as "the sins of his youth," and the few which critical contemporaries considered to be "aberrations of his muse," there cannot be another composer to have such a large proportion of his total oeuvre live on in the consciousness of the musical world. Of course attempts have been made to refute this claim, to show an "aversion against the works of the past," as if Beethoven were "nothing more than the exponent of the third and sixth, the leading melody, and the major and minor tonality." It would be equally nonsensical to look at a painting and enquire after the chemical formula of the paint used.

It does not seem possible to establish a standard for judging greatness through the normal channels of human logic, although it is often embedded in what Goethe called "the feeling for proportions that have a unique beauty and are immortal; whose major chords one can demonstrate, but whose secrets can only be felt." Beethoven's "major chords" have been measured, and the conclusion is that their beauty depends on their order, and that they must be the product of "the most profound intellect." Some have even dared to claim that Beethoven was the greatest musician of all time not despite, but because of, his deafness.

No less interesting and puzzling than the works themselves is the controversial picture of Beethoven's life. Although his own belief in the "uniqueness of his destiny" cannot be judged—much as one is tempted to do so at various points—no other composer demands so urgently that we consider the effect of his creations in the light of his own life; the two cannot be separated. It does not seem possible to say with certainty to what extent his works were inspired by literature; they can be understood with or without such aids. "So if we happen to form this or that thought . . . whatever it is, that is what the composer wanted to convey to us. And if we should happen to think of many very different things, it is because he actually wanted to say a great many vastly different, even contradictory things to us . . ." (Georges Duhamel).

It is inconceivable that Beethoven's works should ever cease to enjoy the popularity they deserve, not least because—regardless of any passing fashion—they are so deeply rooted in our civilization. He was a true avantgardiste who devoted his whole life to "moving forward," "refinement," "freedom," and the "true value of art." He is, and remains, the "man who brings joy to millions."

CHRONOLOGY

1770 December 17th: Ludwig, son of Johann and Maria Magdalena van Beethoven, baptized in Bonn.

1774 Beginning of his musical education with his father.

1778 March 26th: first appearance with the court orchestra at an academy concert in Cologne.

1781 Journey to Rotterdam with his mother.

1782 Beginning of his tuition under Neefe. His first compositions.

1783 Publication of the three sonatas dedicated to the Elector. November: concert in The Hague.

1784 Election of Maximilian Franz as Elector of Cologne. Beethoven appointed second court organist.

1787 April: Visit to Vienna—interview with Mozart. Friendship with Count Waldstein. Composition of the *Ritterballet*.

1791 Visit to Bad Mergentheim with the court orchestra. Meeting with Sterkel in Aschaffenburg.

1792 November: Beethoven's second visit to Vienna. Study with Haydn, Schenk, and Salieri. Composition of the String Trio op. 3.

1793 With Haydn to visit Prince Esterházy in Eisenstadt.

1794 Study with Albrechtsberger.

1795 Spring: end of his training. March: first public appearances in Vienna. Publication of op. 1, the three Piano Trios.

1796 February: journey to Prague, Dresden, Leipzig, and Berlin. Meeting with the King of Prussia, Prince Louis Ferdinand, and Zelter. November 23rd: concert in Pressburg. Composition of *Adelaide*.

1797 April 6th: first performance of the String Quintet op. 16.

1798 Beginning of his hearing difficulties. Composition of the *Sonate Pathétique*.

1800 String Quartet op. 18. April 2nd: first academy concert of his own works, including the First Symphony, the Septet op. 20 and a piano concerto. April 18th: concert with the famous horn player, Punto, playing Beethoven's Horn Sonata op. 17. Prince Lichnowsky's legacy.

1801 March 28th: first performance of *Die Geschöpfe des Prometheus* in the Hofburg Theatre. June: death of the Elector Maxmilian Franz.

1802 C. Czerny and F. Ries become his pupils. October: Heiligenstadt Testament.

1803 April 5th: academy concert: Second Symphony, Third Piano Concerto and the oratorio *Christus am Ölberg*. Composition of the *Kreutzer* Sonata. Visit to Ofen. Commission for an opera from Schikaneder.

1804 Beginning of Prince Rudolf's music lessons with Beethoven. Composition of the *Eroica*.

1805 Meeting with Cherubini and Abbé Vogler. April 7th: first performance of the *Eroica*. November 20th: *Fidelio* (first version).

1806 March 29th: *Fidelio* (second version). December 23rd: first performance of the Violin Concerto. Composition of the String Quartets op. 59.

1807 Composition of the Mass op. 86 for Esterházy: Subscription concerts: the Fourth Symphony, the Fourth Piano Concerto, the *Coriolan* Overture.

1808 May: Triple Concerto. Summons from King Jérôme to go to Cassel.

1809 February: contract with the princes. May: bombardment of Vienna. Fifth Piano Concerto and the String Quartet op. 74.

1810 Marriage proposal to Therese Malfatti. Composition of the music for *Egmont*. Meeting with Bettina Bretano.

1811 Letter to Goethe. First visit to Teplitz. Meeting there with Tiedge and Varnhagen van Ense. Performance of the Esterházy mass in Troppau.

1812 February 9th: first performance of the incidental music to *The Ruins of Athens* and *King Stephen* in Pest. Meeting with Goethe. The letter to the "immortal beloved." Composition of the Seventh and Eighth Symphonies. Visit to his brother Johann in Linz.

1813 Meeting with Mälzel, Moscheles, and Meyerbeer. December 8th: *Wellington's Victory* performed in Vienna along with the new symphonies. May 23rd: revival of *Fidelio* (third version). Composition of the Trio for Piano op. 97 and the *Namensfeier* Overture. Death of Prince Lichnowsky.

1815 Concerts in connection with the Congress of Vienna. Death of his brother Karl. Beethoven assumes guardianship of his nephew. Setting of Goethe's *Meeresstille und Glückliche Fahrt.*

1816 Beginning of the litigation over Karl's guardianship. Composition of the song cycle: *An die ferne Geliebte.* Death of Prince Lobkowitz.

1817 He is visited by Marschner. Conversations with Grillparzer. Composition of the Quintet Fugue op. 137.

1818 Broadwood piano presented to Beethoven. Work on the Scottish songs.

1819 Complete deafness; use of "conversation books." Schindler becomes his factotum. Beginning of the *Missa solemnis.* Diabelli's request for a variation of his waltz.

1820 The lawsuit against his brother's widow decided in Beethoven's favor. Meeting with Zelter. Frequently together with his brother Johann. The *Missa solemnis* offered to Simrock.

1821 Jaundice. Piano Sonata op. 110.

1822 Beethoven visited by Rochlitz. Meeting with Rossini and Carl Maria von Weber. First performance of the *Consecration of the House* Overture at the opening of the Josefstadt Theater on October 3rd.

1823 Completion of the *Missa solemnis* and the *Diabelli* Variations. Offer of subscriptions for the *Missa* to all the large courts.

1824 May 7th: important academy concert—the Ninth Symphony and parts of the *Missa.* Composition of the String Quartet op. 127. Publication of the *Missa* by Schott in Mainz.

1825 Friendship with Karl Holz. Composition of the last string quartets. Performance of op. 127 and op. 132.

1826 March 21st: op. 130 given its first performance by Schuppanzigh. Suicide attempt by his nephew. Journey to his brother in Gneixendorf. His last composition: the finale to op. 130. Plans for a tenth symphony. Complete breakdown of his health.

1827 Cirrhosis of the liver diagnosed. Numerous visitors including Franz Schubert. Publication of the *Missa solemnis*. March 26th: death of Ludwig van Beethoven.

BIBLIOGRAPHY

1. Letters and Other Documents

ANDERSON, EMILY, ed. *The Letters of Beethoven*, 3 vols. New York, 1961.

——, ed. *Selected Letters of Beethoven*. New York (paper edition), 1967.

HAMBURGER, MICHAEL. *Beethoven: His Letters, Journals, and Conversations*. London (paper edition), 1966.

KERST, FRIEDRICH. *Beethoven: The Man and the Artist, Revealed in His Own Words*. Translated by Henry E. Krehbiel. New York, 1905.

MACARDLE, DONALD. *Index to Beethoven's Conversation Books*. Detroit, 1962.

——, and MISCH, LUDWIG, eds. *New Beethoven Letters*. Norman, Oklahoma, 1957.

SONNECK, OSCAR G. *Beethoven: Impressions by His Contemporaries*. New York, 1967.

——. *Beethoven Letters in America*. New York, 1927.

2. Biography and Criticism

BORY, ROBERT. *Ludwig van Beethoven: His Life and Work in Pictures*. New York, 1960.

PUGNETTI, GINO. *The Life and Times of Beethoven*. Translated by Laila Pauk. London, 1967.

SCHINDLER, ANTON F. *Beethoven as I Knew Him*. Translated by Constance S. Jolly. Chapel Hill, 1966.

SCHRADE, LEO. *Beethoven in France: The Growth of an Idea*. New Haven, 1942.

SCOTT, MARION. *Beethoven*. New York, 1949.

THAYER, ALEXANDER W. *Life of Beethoven*, 2 vols. New York, revised edition, 1967.

VALENTIN, ERICH. *Beethoven and His World*. New York, 1969.

Perhaps the greatest of all composers, Ludwig van Beethoven has been described as the last of the classicists and the first of the romantics. Music historian Fritz Zobeley gives careful attention to the composer's problems with growing deafness, his disillusionment with the Napoleonic wars, his numerous unhappy love relationships especially with his "immortal beloved," and his final years marked by ill health and the incorrigible behavior of his nephew.

Despite all this, as the author shows, Beethoven was still able to write with an extraordinary abundance, and at no time was there ever any sign that the maturation of his genius showed any serious setback or period of stagnation. Zobeley divides the composer's career into three cycles: the first, up to age thirty-one, when he still followed mainly in the classical heritage left to him by Hayden and Mozart; the middle period, lasting to 1814, when although already beset with deafness, he wrote some of his greatest music—including the Third and Fifth Symphonies, and his opera *Fidelio;* and his final years, marked by increasing interiority and spiritual compassion, when he composed his Ninth Symphony, the *Missa Solemnis,* and his incomparable string quartets.

Additional features include reproductions of many famous portraits of the composer and members of his family and circle of friends. A chronology is provided for handy reference, and the bibliography will prove of especial value to students of musical history and criticism.